WHAM BAM!
NYC IN THE ROARING SIXTIES

Robert "robear" Isenberg

© 2021 All rights to text and images are reserved by FairlyFamous Press and Robert Isenberg

ISBN: 978-0-578-42141-4

Robert Isenberg, Lexington, MA

Advance Praise for
WHAM BAM! NYC IN THE ROARING SIXTIES

Erma Bombeck once said, "There is a thin line that separates laughter and pain, comedy and tragedy, humor and hurt. Author Robert Isenberg's book, WHAM BAM! NYC IN THE ROARING SIXTIES, is a truly one of a kind comedy with themes of steamy romances and take hold absurd and outrageous characters that readers can't help but be interested in.

Steven Stone, Book Reviewer, Pearson Media Group

An entertaining, interesting memoir which is strengthened by the personable, engaging authorial voice. There is a striking honesty to the anecdotal style that allows the reader to elate inthe joys and share in the challenges. It is written in an accessible, immersive manner with detailed context that
transports the reader into the author's personal journey as well as his career. It is an enjoyable, inspiring read.

Board of Editors, Austin Macauley Publishers

This book depicts a period of time I missed altogether, havingbeen in law school, followed by four years in the U.S. Army during the Viet Nam epoch. The book is well-written, thoughtful and informative on the interesting and lifestyle changing 60's.I highly recommend the book. I enjoyed the insights and the humor.

George S. Silverman ,Esq.

A wonderful story joining the likes of Seinfeld and Woody Allen.

Saul Beaumont

I needed this snow day to have time to read through your book. It is fabulous. Funny, touching, sentimental and engrossing. Loved every minute.

Laura Goldstein, MEd.

WHAM BAM!
NYC IN THE ROARING SIXTIES

ROBERT "robear" ISENBERG

*For all of us,
who don't know what the hell we are doing,
and still come out okay!!*

Table of Contents

PREFACE 1
1. A FRESH START 4
2. A FRESHER START 21
3. SIZE SHOULD NOT MATTER 26
4. A REAL BUSINESS IN THE MAKING 31
5. THE DELIVERY BOY 37
6. SUE QUESTIONS AND CONFESSES 44
7. SALADS AND SARDINES 51
8. GETTING TO MEET IRA 57
9. THE SIMON AND GARFUNKEL CONCERT 64
10. LLOYD'S 73
11. ABBIE HOFFMAN OFFERS ME MY FIRST JOINT 79
12. LEARNING ABOUT BARS 87
13. NATASHA THE WAITRESS 95
14. DICK AND SKIP TELL ME ABOUT BRANDY'S 103
15. MY BROTHER LOU MAKES HIS ENTRANCE 109
16. MY DAD CHECKS IN 114
17. ESTHER NAN MAKES HER FIRST APPEARANCE .. 118
18. SUE GETS TO KNOW ABOUT MY FAMILY 122

19. ABBIE HOFFMAN MAKES AN OFFER 134
20. MY SISTER CHARLOTTE AND AN OLD FRIEND 143
21. GOING TO COURT WITH SUE 149
22. ABBIE IS RELENTLESS 159
23. THE GIRLS THAT STUFFED ARE BACK 163
24. THE FRANCHISE PROPOSAL 173
25. SANDY AND I CUT A DEAL 178
26. THE PROFESSOR TEACHES ME SAICHEL 187
27. CHARLIE IS LOOKING FOR THE MISSING BOTTLE OF VODKA 199
28. I FINALLY MOVE 215
29. A WALK IN THE PARK 223
30. THE BOTTLE OF VODKA IS FOUND 232
31. MADGA, SUE, AND PALATSCHINKE 238
32. JAKE BRINGS A DATE 255
33. DIANE AND I GO TO THE MOVIES 263
34. THE LAST SANDWICH 274
EPILOGUE 282
ADDENDUM. FRED 289

PREFACE

I HAVE WRITTEN this book to leave a recording of my Sixties experiences in New York City, where "it" wasall happening. Change was in the air. Some of it positive;some of it not so positive. New York City was the mecca. The 'City' was the place to be if you were lucky enough tobe there, especially in the Village that celebrated songsters and fresh, young comedy. This telling is true to the time. You will not find "politically correct" in any of the chapters."P.C." had not arrived in the states yet. Most certainly notanywhere in NYC.

People were speaking out. Songs of protest were taking over the radio. There was a breath of freedom in the air. It was a breath of hope. People believed that there could be change. Negro voices could be heard and possibly listened to. We actually were convinced that a better world was coming.

There was the miracle of sex. Girls were doing it! There was the birth control pill. Join me and meet the women I was lucky enough to get to know and learn from.However, marriage was unthinkable. Why would anyone want to get married? We were married to NYC!

There was attitude. No one was going to set the rules for this generation again, certainly not any older person. "Don't Trust Anyone Over Thirty!" was the cry that resonated throughout us.

Yet, there was the tragedy of war. America was mercilessly bombing the very small country of North Vietnam. Young men and women were going to fight battles there. Few of us were ever sure why. Many of the warriors never came home.

At home, young men and women were going down south to help register black voters. In the process, too many lost their lives and even more lost their dreams.

Most of my story takes place uptown, much of it in a strange bar called Lloyd's. There I met with many fascinating people. Some were old friends, and some were new friends like Abbie Hoffman. It was in Lloyd's that I made Robert's Fairly Famous Roast Beef Sandwiches: "NOT ONLY ARE MY SANDWICHES ILLITERATE, BUT THEY'RE THICK". It was in Lloyd's that opportunities presented themselves.

Take this journey with me. Recall songs from the Sixties as they blare out from the well-used jukebox at Lloyd's. Meet some of the writers of that time, many of whom would become famous celebrities.

Discover with me the Thalia theatre on the upper

West Side. It specialized in playing early American or foreign films, when most theatres only showed current Hollywood movies. Often films were shown for "one night only", heightening our awareness of the unique possibility of each moment.

Sit back and remember where you were in the Sixties. Even if you missed them, you can still sit back and think about where you would have been in the Sixties had you been there.

1
A FRESH START

I WAS VERY young and very horny, but also very, very shy. *A bad combination.*

I had arrived in New York City in March, from Boston. It was now September. Pat had just left to go back to the University of Michigan. She liked to call it the "Harvard of the Midwest."

I was lucky with Pat. I met her at a party. I probably had enough to drink to carry on a decent conversation. She liked me instantly and drove me back to my apartment in her brand-new black Chrysler convertible. Her dad bought it for her nineteenth birthday as a "small present" for all of her school success. She had planned to spend two weeks sight-seeing in Manhattan. She ended up spending the entire summer in my apartment on East 85th Street. I would definitely miss her. She was a great cook. I believe her mother was Hungarian. The beef stroganoff Pat made once a week was proof enough for me. Hungarian or not, she had been my first live-in girlfriend. I loved knowing that no matter how my day had gone, she would be there when I arrived home.

Since I was a shallow human being, another reason that I would miss Pat was that she was a real blonde and beautiful. She had a pair of full-bodied breasts. Large breasts for me were basically meaningless. It had never mattered to me sexually whether a girl had small, medium, or large breasts. I never really understood why size mattered. But I was flattered when my acquaintances would salivate over Pat. They would whisper, "What a pair of lungs!", "How did you manage to get her?", "She's gorgeous!"

My friend Jake, who had been my savior, joined us for many of these dinners that Pat cooked. I arrived in NYC knowing no one but Jake. Actually, I only slightly knew Jake. Even though he grew up near me in Dorchester, a suburb of Boston, we had never done anything together. Somehow, I had his phone number and he kindly offered me a couch to sleep on until I found my own place. Although his apartment was not spacious, Jake made room for me. Also, he had developed an uncanny ability to find ethnic restaurants that treated us to the very best of their homeland cuisines for very little money. I thought Jake was a treasure. Pat was not so sure. I thought Pat just wanted me all to herself.

Jake annoyed Pat because, after every dating experience, he would say the same thing, "That girl was incredibly fucked up!!" We never even got as far as their names. Pat mentioned more than once, "They can't all be incredibly fucked up."

In fact, we had fixed Jake up with Pat's supposed friend Nancy, who had whispered to me that she wanted to sleep with me. When I told Pat, she thought that at least proved that Nancy wasn't incredibly fucked up, she was just a little fucked up.

Pat was not only beautiful and a great cook. While I was at work, she would discover amazing events throughout the city, almost all free of charge. We saw many, many soon-to-be stars, just as their careers were beginning to begin. New York city was our very own land full of wonders.

Because of Pat's sharp perusing, we caught Woody Allen at The Bitter End accusing an elevator of being anti- Semitic. After admiring Woody Allen's stand-up routine, I looked at Pat and said, "You know he's very funny, but I think most of us with a little imagination could do just as well as that nerd."

Pat grinned. "Oh yeah, did you hear the audience clamoring for more? The other thing that occurred to me is you don't have to be Jewish to laugh along with him."

"Maybe so, but where is Mr. Woody going to go from here in the Village?" I looked back at Pat.

She somehow got us in early at The Village Gate to hear Bob Dylan and Joan Baez, singing Dylan's songs of protest. We blended in with the packed room. We felt we belonged. Dylan's lyrics struck a chord.

"G-D, he's probably close to my age. I wish to hell I could write like that. He's beyond brilliant."

Pat exclaimed, "You know he's from Minnesota. I wonder if he ever came to Michigan? G-D they would have loved him at my school."

With a sly smile Pat touched my leg and continued, "Yes, I agree he's brilliant, but there is something unsettling about him. Something unsettling about his music as well. I hate that I feel so guilty after listening to his lyrics. I'm guessing he'd be very hard to live with."

Because of Pat's nose for local happenings, we got to see and hear Neil Diamond sing in Central Park. The crowd was so raucous that the police came with billy clubs to break up the party.

We were there when Lenny Bruce got arrested with his opening monologue that included a few profanities. It took place at The Fillmore East on the lower East Side. It was later turned into a recording studio for famous rock and roll singers like Linda Ronstadt.

Pat spotted that both Tony Bennett and Jack Jones would be performing further north at a place called Freedom Land. While Tony Bennett was singing, someone kept yelling at Tony, "Go back to San Francisco. You can't sing."

Pat fell in love with Jack Jones's very blue eyes. He also stared at her throughout his whole repertoire.

On the way home, Pat remarked, "That was a helluva lot different than the Village crowd, but if the music is good, I'm fine with being square and sitting with squares."

Pat drew a square in the air and smiled. "Did you notice Jack Jones staring at me?"

"I did notice. I also noticed you smiling back at him. I was getting jealous."

Pat reached over. "You don't have to ever be jealous of anyone. You are my guy. I love you. Even if you can't sing." Pat laughed.

It was one more summer evening of being entertained and enjoying each other's company to the fullest. But fall was looming.

My glorious summer was over. Pat had left. I wouldn't go hungry, but I would miss her. I'd miss the way her smooth soft arms hugged me all night, so much so that I would wish the night would go on all day. As she was departing, Pat had insisted that I promise not to wear short sleeve shirts because she thought my arms were very attractive. She also asked me not to date anyone else. All I had left was a horrible job, Jake's description of his disastrous dates, and long sleeve shirts. What to do?

I stopped this self-pity as soon as I thought about what I'd read in the previous day's article in the Herald Tribune. It was about people, some my age, going to the "South," trying to help negroes register to vote. Some of them were called "Freedom Riders." The article stated that even if they chose to ride a simple Greyhound bus, they could be brutally beaten with sticks and pipes, or even killed by their fellow Americans. Frequently these Freedom Riders were jailed. They were jailed by the local police for having put their friends, the good citizens, to the trouble of doing these beatings. It was hard for me to envisage this. Could this be my America? Is this what my brothers had fought for? What could I do, if anything, except feel guilty?

However, soon after Pat left, as I was rushing out of my building, Sue traipsed right by me. She turned, smiled and asked, "You live here don't you?"

I smiled back. "Yes, on the third floor. I won't ask what you do. I can see your TWA uniform."

Sue retorted, "I had a feeling you were pretty sharp."

"You must have just landed, right?"

Sue continued, "You have it all together, don't you? What cell are you in?"

"310," I answered.

"Wow! I'm right over you. I'm in 410. No wonder I've been sleeping so well. For a change I got home earlier than usual, and my plan was to make my famous marinara sauce over whatever pasta I had on the shelf. I had been planning to eat alone, which I hate doing. Would love to have you join me."

I chuckled. "Wow, yourself. What a left-handed invite that is. Are you saying anyone is better than eating alone?"

"Hey, don't get all prissy on me. I'll try again. Please join me for dinner tonight in my exquisite abode at about 6:30."

"On one condition . . . the next time you are home early enough for dinner, you'll come all the way down to my simply furnished apartment, 310, and join me and my fairly famous roast beef for supper. I've been buying this incredible cut of roast beef at Mario's Meat Market on First Avenue. I went in there a few weeks ago and I overheard this young woman say to Mario, 'I'm trying to snare this doctor. I need your help. He loves roast beef. Please, please give me your very best, special cut of roast beef.'

"After she left, I told Mario, 'I'll have whatever you sold her even though I've no intention of getting married.' Mario seemed to nod knowingly."

Sue put out her hand for me to shake. "You made yourself a deal my new friend."

I watched Sue get on the elevator. Wow! Wow! Wow! is the right word. Sue, a beautiful red-headed flight attendant, had just invited me to dinner.

Best of all, this couldn't be considered a real date, since we weren't really going out. I was still being true to Pat. I knew two things for sure: I would not invite Jake to join us and I wouldn't mention it to Pat.

***

I made sure that I got home from work early. Dinner with Sue would be at 6:30. I needed at least an hour to figure out what to talk to Sue about. I was not happy with myself to say the least.

I hated my job. I couldn't possibly talk about it. I usually finished the entire week's work on Monday morning by 11:00. I took to walking around the building and checking on the other people in the other cubbyhole offices. It was depressing. Most of them were old. They were all in their forties or fifties, doomed to spend their entire lives in this prison. Would that happen to me too? I had no idea what to say to these people. Most of them had kids older than me. Mostly they talked about the barbecues they had on Sunday, how much beer got consumed, and who ate the most hot dogs. Would this happen to me?

I didn't want to talk about school. I had gone to a premier high school—Boston Latin—but had really only excelled in the ninth grade when I received approbation with distinction. College was worse. I slept through most of the classes that I didn't cut. I was severely depressed and painfully shy. What I didn't know was how severe my learning disabilities were. I had severe ADD, but

"Attention Deficit Disorder" wasn't even a concept then. I have since thought my ADD was linked to my oldest brother getting killed in the war when I was six. I believe that I preferred my daydreams to the reality of my household.

Yet what would I talk with Sue about? I was at a loss.

We'll have to see, I told myself.

The next debate I had with myself was *should I arrive early? No! That would be showing I was overanxious. Should I be cool and arrive a little late? Sue probably wouldn't even notice.*

I rang her bell at exactly 6:30. Sue opened the door with a big smile. She was wearing an apron boldly embroidered with her first and last name, **Sue Cassidy**. I got a better look at her. She had that kind of skin redheads usually come with, very white and spotted with a few freckles. It was the same beautiful face I had seen in the lobby. *What did I expect?* I laughed to myself.

"Come in. Welcome. Make yourself comfortable. Dinner will be ready in a jiff."

"Smells good."

I took in her place. Exactly the same as mine, of course, but look what she had done with it! Everything was in its place. There was a soft and inviting couch. There were a few wicker chairs that all seemed to be saying, "Sit on me. I'm even more comfortable than I look." They all had cushy, cushy cushions on their seats.

And there was no clutter.

Sue called out, "Dinner is ready!"

I had just sat down when Sue began, "Do you have a girlfriend?"

"Well, sort of," I lied. "She went back to school last week."

"Was she the blond with 'big bazookas'? I saw her a few times at the front door."

"That's the one."

"She didn't work?"

"No, she's a student."

"University of Michigan? Right?"

"How did you know that?"

"One time I saw her in the lobby, primping away, wearing a University of Michigan sweater. I hated her! I had my TWA uniform on. She seemed to smirk at me. Did you like her? I mean, did you really like her?"

"Of course, I liked her. I spent the whole summer with her."

"Well, that tells me nothing. I spend a lot of hours in the air with a whole lot of people I don't like. I suspect you were with her for other reasons."

"I'm not sure that when you are sleeping with someone, you spend a lot of time thinking if you like them."

"Here's the thing. Most people think stewardesses are very stupid. What they don't realize is how much we have to learn in order to do our job. We have to spend a ton of hours getting prepared for just about anything that could possibly happen. What they don't prepare us for is that, just about on every flight, at least three or four guys ask me out. I usually accept one invite. Why not? They almost always take me to the best restaurants. I'd be foolish to say no. I have to listen to how hard it is to be married with kids and have to travel. They usually go on about how beautiful I am. Of course, I don't agree. By the way, I really don't agree. Then they get to the point. They ask where I live, and can they take me home."

Sue put some more marinara sauce in the bowl.

"Sue, I have to agree with those guys. I think you are very beautiful and especially nice, but maybe a little 'air headed.' Get the joke? Anyway, once these men have treated you to a delicious dinner, complimented you in many ways, they want to take you home. So, what's the big deal? I took many a girl home in Dorchester and sadly not much happened."

I munched on the Italian loaf Sue served with the pasta.

Sue ranted, "You are the 'air head'! What do you think they want? Where did you try to grow up? Anyway, my point is when someone like that treats you to compliments, they do it for their own benefit. I have a feeling your Pat 'gone to Michigan girlfriend' did the same thing with you, just maybe a little differently. I'll bet she 'flowered' you with so many compliments, you smelled only roses. I'm guessing, of course, but I think she took ownership of you and your very soul."

She pushed the marinara sauce closer to my plate.

"Hey, you and I just met. Maybe you saw Pat once or twice, and you and I are just beginning to talk. Or, might I say, you are talking and I'm listening. How can you surmise all of this without knowing either one of us?"

"If you remember, I 'suspected.' But my guess is, if it were for real, she would have dropped out of the University of Michigan. She would have enrolled at N.Y.U., or you would have followed her and found a job at Ann Arbor. Anyway, let's drop Pat for the while and talk about you, your hopes, and aspirations." Sue looked up from her plate. "Let me also add that I'm glad you didn't go to Michigan, it's frightfully cold there." Sue faked a shiver.

I scratched my head. "I'm curious. What do flight attendants have to know? Where do you get taught stuff?"

"We have to know what to do in an emergency landing or any emergency for that matter. Use your imagination 'city boy.' Your Pat went back to the University of Michigan. Right? What the hell is she going to learn? Oh yeah, she'll read a few books. What is she going to do with all that 'hoity toity' stuff? How many lives are in her hands every day?"

Sue snickered.

"I thought you wanted to drop Pat. Where did you

say you grew up?"

Sue laughed. "I didn't say. Somewhere over the rainbow, how is that for a hint? I'll give you one more. Dorothy wanted to go back. I don't. I like it here. Anyway, what is your best guess?"

"Topeka, Kansas."

Sue laughed again. "I was thinking of singing a few bars of *I'm as corny as Kansas in August*, but I didn't want to make it too easy for a sharp 'city boy' like you. How is my marinara sauce?"

"Delicious. Yum, the best. More please."

Sue smiled. "You know what's good for you, don't you 'city boy'?"

"By the way, I'm no 'city boy.' I have spent most of my life in a suburb of Boston called Dorchester. No high rises. Not many restaurants, if any. Not even a sub shop that I can remember. We had one thing of note: a bagel factory. People came from all over for those bagels. They later branched out to many places. Finally, they went broke. One of the brothers had his hand in the till and his heart at the track. Lost everything—every single bagel. Yeah, more sauce please, it's delicious."

I smacked my lips.

"Were the bagels any good? We didn't have bagels in Topeka. You know that I grew up without ever having a bagel. I didn't miss them even once."

"They were the best, none better. If you had ever had one of these bagels, you'd miss them. New York City brags about its bagels. They couldn't touch these Dorchester bagels."

I patted my stomach.

Sue murmured, "What was Dorchester like?"

"Not much to tell about it. We played a lot of ball games. Different ones each season. When I think back to what I thought was important then, it is ridiculous to me now. I cared about winning every single game. When I think back, I say what difference did it make then or does it make now?"

I met Sue's gaze.

"I don't follow sports. They bore me for the most part. Did you have a girlfriend?" Sue wanted to know.

"No, I was in love with the girl next door, but I wasn't even allowed to speak to her. It wouldn't have made a difference even if my mother let me talk to her. She was older, beautiful, and snotty. She wouldn't have given me the time of day. Her name was Ruthie."

"Why wouldn't your mother allow you to speak to her?" Sue got up to go to the kitchen.

"That's another story. I was sort of friendly with her younger brother. As I best recall, his name was Louis. Anyway, Louis came down with the German measles. His mother didn't tell my mother. She invited me over to play with Louis. Hey, I'm going back a thousand years, maybe I'm not exactly correct. What are you getting in the kitchen?"

"Well, if Louis's mother did do that, I don't blame

your mom for exiling them."

Sue was back from the kitchen with more pasta.

"It was miserable living right next door to their house and not being allowed to even say hello." I sighed. "But, yes, I'll have more pasta and sauce."

"Tell me all about Ruthie," Sue said with a grin as she rubbed her legs.

"Really not much to tell. I never spoke two words to her. What I did frequently was mow my lawn between the two houses and sing *You Alone, You Alone Are the Dream I Have Known*. At the time it was a smash hit by Perry Como. Ruthie would dangle her smooth legs over the porch's banister, and I would drool onto the grass. This was before power mowers. At least, we didn't have one. So, Ruthie could hear my mournful, pathetic singing."

"Love you to sing a few bars to me." Sue grinned again.

"Next time. Remember we have a roast beef date at my place."

"Believe me, I have not forgotten. I love roast beef. I can't wait to find out how good a chef you are. Remember, I get taken to a lot of 'hoity toity' places."

"My place may not be considered 'hoity toity,'" I admitted, "but I can't wait for you to taste my cooking."

"Speaking of 'hoity toity,' I apologize for coming down so hard on Pat. It's probably universal with me. Like I told you, the world calls us 'stews.' Some think we are not bright. I had a feeling Pat gave me that look. I admit that I'm paranoid about it and overly defensive. I've actually gone to parties where I've been insulted about what I do."

Sue pouted.

"I've gone to parties where I have just been insulted, never mind what I do. Pat was very proud of her scholarly prowess. She frequently liked to use bigger words than necessary. Hey, we all have our shortcomings, except you and me."

I sat up in my chair.

Sue laughed. "Except maybe me. Anyway, Dorchester sounds as boring as Topeka, except for the bagels and Ruthie's legs."

Sue continued to pat her legs.

"What about Topeka?" I prodded.

"Well, my mom and dad have been married forever. They were great parents—always trying to teach my brother and me right from wrong. I did my best not to be a quick study. Can't speak for my brother Steve. I think my parents preferred names beginning with 'S.' Pretty boring so far, right? Listen to this. It gets worse. My dad called my mom 'sweetie,' or 'honey,' and sometimes even 'honey-bug.' I know. Don't gag. But it allowed him to tell his favorite joke. Once somebody asked him, 'You two have been married for forty-five years, how come you are still using all those affectionate terms after all these years?' My dad replied, 'When you get to my age you have no memory left. Please don't tell my wife that I forgot her name.'"

Sue giggled.

"Sue, it sounds to me that it's our turn to have a lot of excitement. What do you say?"

I handed my empty dish to Sue. Sue yawned as she headed back to the kitchen.

"I'm all in. I'm also all in for the evening. I had a grueling day, plus making that incredibly perfect marinara sauce took the starch out of me."

"Okay, I'll go down to my place empty handed. *Don't think twice* as Bob Dylan croons."

Sue smiled widely. "I'll be there at 6:30, Thursday. I warn you right now, I'm a very hungry girl on Thursdays."

As I left, I could hear Sue running the water in the kitchen sink.

2

A FRESHER START

I GOT HOME early on Thursday and had luckily picked up a three-pound special cut of roast beef on Wednesday. The plan was to cook it at about twenty minutes a pound for medium rare results. I had forgotten to ask Sue how she liked her meat, but I was going to bet on the rare side.

I made one of my salads that had always received rave reviews and even concocted my very own salad dressing: olive oil, dill, lemon, and grated Parmesan cheese. I cut up some potatoes extremely thin and placed them in the oven, again with a lot of olive oil. They would come out in about an hour as homemade potato chips. I opened a bottle of red wine since I'd heard red went with roast beef. I also heard that it was best to let it breathe on the table right beyond the kitchen.

Back in Dorchester, we had a rib roast just about every Sunday. My mother added a Yorkshire pudding, salad, and a veggie of sorts. It never mattered how well my dad was faring. It was a ritual. I usually helped set the table and stirred the salad. Then I would sit patiently waiting for one of my older siblings to arrive with their broods. There was never any wine, but there was plenty of noise. I had thirteen nieces and nephews. They were not quiet.

I thought I was pretty well prepared for Sue. I knew food. My doorbell rang. I looked at my watch—it was 6:29. Sue was one minute early. She couldn't wait to see me. I smiled to myself.

Sue exclaimed as she picked up the bottle of wine to look at the label, "Smells awfully good in here. What's cooking? Hey, how did you know I could use a glass of wine? Can't wait to try it!"

"I'll answer all your questions one by one. I'm cooking the roast beef I promised. Actually, it's ready. I'm roasting very thinly cut potatoes that you are going to love. As far as the wine, I was hoping you would want more than one glass of this vintage wine. Anyway, I'm guessing you had a rough day today."

I put the two wine glasses that Pat had bought on the table, along with the uncorked bottle of wine. Pat had been very proud of the wine glasses.

"Rough would have been good! We had a ton of turbulence. There was this old guy . . . I couldn't get him to sit down. The bumpier it got, the more he got up. The smokers were at their worst today. I really couldn't breathe. I must stink of smoke. Yes, fill my glass with that beautiful-looking red."

Sue reached toward me with one of the glasses. I took it and returned it full to the brim. She was almost gulping it down.

I declared, "We need a toast."

I filled my empty glass with that beautiful looking red.

Sue raised her glass and touched my glass ever so gently. "Friends until we die. That roast beef better be good, or I'll take that toast back." Sue took another long sip.

I bragged, "I guarantee you will love every morsel, or I promise to give you double your money back."

Sue moved towards my kitchen. "Can I help you with anything?"

"Now you ask. I've been slaving in this tiny kitchen all day, while you've been taking joy rides around the country. Let's eat."

I brought the roast out of the kitchen, settling it center on my table.

Sue looked at it and said, "That looks perfect!"

I clinked my glass against Sue's glass. I began slicing and putting pieces of the beef on Sue's plate. I brought over the potatoes and salad for Sue to help herself.

Sue began to eat everything that I had placed in front of her.

"Where have you been all my life? You can cook! I mean really cook! This is yummy, delicious. Where did you learn to cook so well?"

"Self-taught like everything I do." I cut a piece of roast beef for myself.

"You ought to do something with this talent," Sue remarked.

"I've already started. I'm calling it 'Robert's Fairly Famous Roast Beef.' I made up a bunch of posters at work. The woman who runs the printer likes me and ran off one hundred posters. I've made a lot of female friends at the 92nd Street 'Y.' They will stuff local mailboxes for me and deliver sandwiches, while I prepare more sandwiches. There are tons of young people living around here. They are busy. They don't want to cook. This is a fabulous service I'm offering."

"I love it! Will you marry me when you get very rich, so I don't have to fly anymore? By the way, when we are finished eating, let's go back up to my place and make love. I don't want to wake up in a strange bed."

Sue finished her second glass of wine.

"You think I'm that easy? You think I'll just say 'Yes,' and then say what a great idea?"

I laughed as Sue put her empty glass in the sink. Sue smiled.

"I do believe you will say 'Yes.' Not only that. I've got another idea. Since your apartment is right under mine, when I come home at night after one of those fancy meals that one of my passengers will no doubt treat me to, I'll just stomp on the floor for you to come up. How does that sound?"

"Well, I have to admit you are very correct. I'm more than that easy."

I grinned as I pushed myself away from the table.

3

SIZE SHOULD NOT MATTER

I STARTED TO pick up a couple of the dishes when Sue jumped up.

"Let me handle the clean-up. I'm good at it and quick. I've seen enough guys struggle over the sink. Besides, you prepared dinner with no help from me."

I watched as Sue cleaned up everything in no time and somehow knew where to put things away. At least, she knew for the most part.

"I suppose you learned how to do clean-up like this in stewardess training."

Sue folded the dish towel, then smiled.

"No, my mom taught me. Let's go upstairs."

As I closed my door, I heard the phone ringing. Must be Pat, I thought. We hadn't had a very pleasant conversation the last time we spoke. Maybe she was calling to apologize for a sour mood or for something that was bugging her. I quickly followed Sue out the door. As soon as we got up to Sue's, we both began yanking our clothes off. I noticed Sue seemed a little hesitant with her top clothes. I was watching Sue so closely I wasn't paying close enough attention to myself. Sure enough because of all my excitement my penis got caught in the zipper. "Oww!"

"Need any help?" she offered.

"I'm okay, just a slight traffic jam. Do you need any help?"

"Not really. It's just . . . well, to tell the truth, I was thinking of Pat's 'big bazookas' and mine are very tiny as you'll soon see." Sue looked over at me shyly.

"Don't be even a tiny bit concerned. Big or small, I'm a devoted breast admirer. Let me unhook your bra and I'll get to see all your loveliness."

"I'll do it myself. You make me feel a lot better. I couldn't get Pat's big breasts out of my mind."

Sue dropped her bra on the floor. Sue was beautiful from top to bottom. Her skin was a perfect off white and totally flawless, except for a few tiny freckles that no doubt came with her sparkling red hair. Her breasts were small, but they were wonderfully firm and pointed upwards in the direction of the ceiling. I called them "little uppies." I promptly planted two gentle kisses on each pink nipple. Sue was pleased and began moaning, as I began caressing and kissing her entire beautiful body.

"I'm just getting started," I whispered.

Her moans finally reached a very loud, exquisite, crescendo of screams that were truly music to my ears.

"Oh, my G-D," Sue gasped.

The movies would have called for a cigarette, but I knew that Sue detested smoke.

I gently touched Sue's hand.

I whispered, "Thank you. What a precious moment. I don't believe I'll ever want to leave your bed. Speaking of precious moments that yell you heard was because my zipper attacked my penis."

"Ouch" Sue cried. "I hate to ask you to leave, but I have a killer day tomorrow. Three stops before we get to Saint Louis and then back to LaGuardia. I've got to get some sleep. And boy, did you ever help. But before you go, next time we get together, I want to ask you if you know anything about that wailing and moaning that seems to be coming from your floor."

Sue seemed exasperated. I knew what she was talking about.

"I know it's frightening and some nights it keeps me awake. I believe it's a very old woman. I may have spotted her once creeping out of her apartment. She didn't look well. In fact, not well at all. Anyway, I know when I'm not wanted. By the way, speaking of moans . . ."

I laughed as I started toward the door.

"Actually, that's the problem. You are wanted, but I've got to get some sleep. Sleep well, my friend, and don't forget to listen for floor stomps."

I stumbled down to my place. As I opened the door, the phone rang. It was Pat.

"I've been calling all night. Where were you? It's late," Pat scolded.

"I was out with Jake," I lied. "We were having a few drinks at a local cool bar called Lloyd's, named after Lloyd Bridges. We met some fun characters there."

I gripped the phone tightly in my hand. Pat went on. I thought I heard her rustling some papers.

"I hope for both our sakes you develop some more friendships, with others than Jake. Did he tell you about any 'totally fucked up girls' he's taken out lately? And how is your horrible job going?"

"Horribly, but I've got an idea for a business that when I know more about it, I'll tell you."

I moved the phone to my other ear.

"I can't wait. Anyway, glad you are okay and that you and Jake had a good time. But I am serious. You need better friends to help you develop more as a person. Sort of like some of the ones I have here at Ann Arbor. We call ourselves the P.P.P. Group for Politics. Poetry. Prose. Each guy is totally brilliant, whether their specialty is politics, poetry, or prose. My roommate just broke up with a brilliant writer. She fell for this handsome poet. Believe me, I can see why!"

"Maybe, maybe you are right. But remember, I haven't been in New York for long. Let's see what happens."

I moved the phone back to my original ear.

Pat warned, "You are a 'let's see' sort of guy. I like my guys more aggressive."

I groaned. "I'm off to sleep. It's late and I'm tired."

I had a lot of trouble falling asleep that evening. I felt a little bit bad about lying to Pat, but we hadn't had a decent conversation, since maybe two weeks after she left. *What happened? What happened to her? I was perfect in her eyes in August. Even into the first week of September, I was 'Mr. Right.' Now I'm 'Mr. Do Nothing' with a horrible job. P.P.P., my ass! Just a whole bunch of guys trying to get into her pants with their collection of bullshit. I'll bet I could write circles around them if I tried. P.P.P., my ass! I could throw up.* I lay there getting angrier and angrier. *I know. I'll picture Sue's 'little uppies.' I'm right. The smaller the breast, the more erogenous it is. Closer to the bone, I had always thought.* I could sense myself smiling as I thought of Sue's breasts.

I was actually looking forward to going to work the next day. My mailers would be ready for stuffing. Finally, I dozed off.

4

A REAL BUSINESS

IN THE MAKING

FOR THE VERY first time since I moved to the city, I couldn't wait to get to the office. The office was in the Bronx, a block from Yankee Stadium. The streets were dank and filled with litter. There were very few trees. It depressed me just to look at the office building. This was not a place one would come to for any reason except, as in my case, for a job. The only good things in the area were some decent restaurants, especially a Kosher Jewish deli. This was a sincerely Kosher deli, not just Jewish style like the ones I had loved in Boston. I got in big trouble there when I ordered a Corned Beef and Swiss sandwich. You had to see their faces. They couldn't have been more upset if I had insulted their wives. There was no mixing meat and milk products on their premises!

The other problem with the area concerned your car's tires. I never knew if they would be intact when I went to drive back to Manhattan. They could be slashed or stolen.

I had gotten up early. This would be one of my first on-time days. I practically flew to the mailroom. Gussie was waiting with a big smile.

"Here they are, all one hundred posters. Check them out and see if they are what you asked for."

I looked at the flyers and they looked perfect. ROBERT'S FAIRLY FAMOUS ROAST BEEF SANDWICHES. NOT ONLY ARE THEY ILLITERATE, BUT THEY'RE THICK!!! stood out at the top. I had come up with that ad because throughout the city, there was a chain of hamburger restaurants called Prexy's featuring THE HAMBURGER WITH THE COLLEGE EDUCATION. I had never tried one. I would never trust any food that knew more than me. It might talk back.

My phone number was prominent. The price .85 was right there. The hours to call for home delivery were clearly specified. I was in business!

I didn't know of anyone else in my neighborhood that delivered. The local apartments were full of young singles and a few that were married. All were in a major hurry to go somewhere quick. No one had time to cook. I was on top of something big. Soon I'd be able to quit my job.

I had been working on a plan. I'd leave work early. I had come in a little early this morning and besides, no one would notice. I'd get to Mario, the butcher, and get a small top round roast. Once I placed it in the oven, it would be ready in one hour. The three girls from the "Y" would arrive at about 6:00 p.m., along with Jake. I'd give each one twenty-five flyers and assign streets where they would stuff mailboxes. Realistically, I didn't expect any calls this first night.

I arrived at the butcher's around 5:15 p.m. and sped home to my apartment. As soon as I opened the door, the phone rang. It was Sue.

I snickered. "Did you call up for a sandwich?"

"Yup, I can't wait to take a bite. What kind of rolls did you buy? What are you offering for condiments?"

"Boy, you know how to hurt a guy. Anyway, good questions. I'm not only an amazing cook, but I also know from rolls. The trick to a great sandwich is you want the roll to do as little talking as possible. You want it to be soft, but yet strong enough to hold the sandwich together. Somewhat like your body. I found a bakery that had the perfect roll and a decent price. Regarding condiments, when they call, I'll offer mustard, or my homemade Russian Dressing and a Bermuda onion."

Sue whispered, "What about mayonnaise?"

"There you go putting on your Midwest hat again. Nobody in New York would put mayonnaise on a roast beef sandwich. And I mean nobody."

"Talk about hurting a girl's feelings. I can't help where I come from. And besides, maybe you should give it a try. You might find you like it, 'Mr. Big Shot.' Anyway, I called to wish you good luck on your first night of this exciting venture. I won't stomp tonight. I'm getting in very late and I'm very tired. The wailer kept me up last night. How about you? Did you sleep well?"

"Yes, I did. I fell asleep thinking about your 'little uppies.'"

"Well, well, I'll take that as a compliment, the very first one I've heard tonight. I've got a lot to teach you. Girls like compliments. Trust me they pay off. They pay off big."

"I know I'm a dummy. I need all the help you can give me. Very sorry about the no stomps tonight. Sorry she kept you up last night. Not much we can do is there?"

"I've been thinking about that. Maybe we should talk to our neighbors and see if we can get some sort of petition going."

"Very much appreciate your calling and wishing me the best. Can't wait to see you and hear the next stomp.

I have to get the roast in the oven just in case the phone starts ringing. It could be someone just hungering for a roast beef sandwich."

"Yum!" Sue laughed as she hung up her phone.

The roast was even smaller than I thought. It would cook in an hour. I checked my condiments: mustard, ketchup, and yes, mayo as Sue had mentioned.

I couldn't stop obsessing about Pat. Why didn't I have the balls, the gumption to say it's over? What did I have to lose? Nothing! Did I really want to hear about the P.P.P.s?

Sue was correct that flattery can trap you and seduce you. Pat had spent the summer telling me how great I was. I bought it. I needed it. I had arrived in NYC very much a tortured soul. My self-esteem was at rock bottom, maybe a minus zero. Along came beautiful Pat. *Oh, get over yourself. It could have happened to any guy. Now do something about it. Let's make something of yourself and your new business.*

Jake was the first to arrive. He had his usual, same, shit-eating grin on his face. Jake sniffed.

"Smells wonderful! Where are the girls? Remind me again, who they are? I can't remember what they look like. Did I ever meet them?"

"Yes, we both met them at the 'Y' . . . Sandy, Lois, and Donna, all very attractive and very nice."

"Great, just like we planned, I'll hand out twenty-five posters to each one and assign them a street to stuff. I'll take one route myself. What the hell are you going to do? I hope you aren't going to sit around thinking about Pat. You know, I never told you before, but Pat was just like all of my dates, incredibly fucked up, only more so. And her father, giving a nineteen-year-old a brand-new Chrysler convertible? Talk about a fucked-up family. Forget her. Consider yourself very lucky. Hey, what's going on with Sue, you know the redhead upstairs?"

Jake pointed at the ceiling. I grinned.

"We are having a stomping good time."

Just as Jake was asking, "What does that mean?" the three girls came in the door Jake had left open. I had been about to tell Jake that I'd wait at the apartment to see if we got any phone calls. If we did, I'd deliver the very first "Robert's Fairly Famous Roast Beef sandwich."

"Hi, ladies, I'm sure you all remember Jake. He's going to tell you where to stuff. By the way, thanks a whole lot for coming over and taking on this task."

5
THE DELIVERY BOY

"**WE ARE REALLY** happy about getting you started. It's so exciting to help a friend, especially because you are so young. Twenty-two, right?" asked Lois.

Lois seemed to be speaking for the three girls.

"We can't wait to get one of those roast beef sandwiches when we return."

"Really, I'm twenty-three, but I wanted to start this business at twenty-two. I just wasn't here to do it. I'm running a year behind. I've got to hurry to catch up."

I grinned as I continued, "I'm going to give each girl twenty-five flyers so we have to be careful not to do every building, just the ones that look like young people might live there."

Jake handed Donna, Lois, and Sandy twenty-five flyers each and kept twenty-five for himself.

Jake declared, "Let's wrap this up as quickly as possible. We'll leave 'Mr. Delivery Boy' here. Let's hope for all our sakes he gets some calls."

I nodded. "If by some miracle I get a call to deliver and I'm out when you return, you know where everything is. If I'm not here, you can make the sandwiches."

"Okay, chief. Good luck," Jake grunted.

Jake waved, called goodbye, and all three scurried out the door.

I began to wonder why it had taken Jake so long to give me his slant on Pat. He certainly loved her cooking and was always very happy to be invited to dinner. It wasn't like Jake to hold off any of his thoughts, particularly regarding "incredibly fucked-up" women.

The phone rang. Could I be that lucky so soon?

"Hi, it's me, Pat, calling from freezing-ass cold Ann Arbor. What's going on? What are you up to?"

"Nothing much."

I wasn't going to tell Pat about the business I had just begun, not until it really got off the ground.

"Well, a lot is going on here," affirmed Pat. "Remember I told you about the Three Ps: Politics, Poetry, and Prose? Well, this really cute leader of the political group found out that President Kennedy started the Peace Corps right here at the University of Michigan. The President also calls it the 'Harvard of the Midwest.' Jacoby is so smart. I already mentioned his name. It's

Jacoby, but he says 'just call me J'.' I love hearing him go on about anything at all. So, have you taken my advice and looked for new friends? A fresh group of friends will help you grow as a person."

"Appreciate your concern for my persona, but right now I'm expecting a call from someone who mentioned they wanted to interview me. I'm not expecting it to amount to anything, but I want to listen. Talk soon," I murmured.

"Hey there, good luck. Hope something will come of it."

Damn! I've got to end these calls. They only piss me off.

I checked the roast. I wanted to make sure that it stayed a tiny bit warm. I picked up the Herald Tribune and had just started Jimmy Breslin's column when the phone rang.

"Hi, is this Robert's Fairly Famous Roast Beef shop?" a girl's voice inquired.

"You got me!"

"Great!" she purred. "I want three of your juiciest roast beef sandwiches. I want them to be thick, just like your ad brags. I'm here on the north east corner of 94th and 5th. My apartment is 10 C. There is a doorman. Tell him you want to come up to deliver sandwiches to Lauren and her friend, Biffy. The third sandwich is for my boyfriend, so they better be good. My boyfriend isn't here yet, but he will be, if he knows what's good for him!

Put a touch of Russian dressing on all three. No Bermuda onions on any. My boyfriend would probably order an onion, but I don't want him stinking up the place."

I took the tiny weight scale and weighed out meat for all three sandwiches at a quarter pound each, added to each a touch of Russian dressing. They looked delicious in their rolls. I wrapped them up. I was on my way.

It was a balmy fall evening. The temperature was an improbable sixty-seven. It should be a nice brisk walk. I calculated that I should be able to get there in twelve minutes. I thought Jake could take care of any new orders, if they were called in to my newly installed answering service before I returned.

I arrived at her building in fifteen minutes. As I began to enter, the doorman approached. He was meticulously dressed in a greenish uniform. I looked up at the commanding cap that fit perfectly on his head. He looked at me and then at my bag that was carrying the sandwiches.

"Yes?" He motioned me toward him with his hand. "And what might you be wanting?" he asked, with a hint of a brogue.

"I'm delivering sandwiches to Lauren and her girlfriend up in 10 C."

I didn't mention that there was also one for her boyfriend.

"Ah, indeed. They had better be good, mind you, or Lauren will give me holy hell for letting you in. If they are not, she's a devil that one. But if she likes them, I'll know that too. If she does, next time you can bring me one. How much are you getting for a sandwich?"

"Eighty-five cents," I offered.

"Reasonable, very reasonable, mind you if they are any good. Anyway, good luck with Lauren. Be sure to tell her my hello. The elevator is on your left. Make sure to press the 10 button."

He saluted me and pointed to the door. I didn't salute back. I hurried to the elevator. I didn't want the sandwiches to get cold. When I reached the apartment, I rang Lauren's doorbell.

A girl's voice yelled, "I'm coming! Hold your horses!!"

Lauren opened the door. She grinned.

"You must be the sandwich man. Come in."

I hurried through the open door.

"Hope the sandwiches are still nice and warm," I told them.

Lauren looked me up and down. "He doesn't look much like a delivery boy, does he?"

She looked over at her friend and continued, "Are you Robert? Are you Fairly Famous?"

"Yes, I'm both."

"Well, I'll call you 'Fairly.' By the way, where do these sandwiches come from? Did you make them yourself?"

I answered, "85th Street and yes, I made them myself."

"How long have you lived at 85th?"

"About three months," I responded.

"Soooo, where did you live before 85th Street?" Lauren cooed.

"Boston—Boston, Mass," I replied.

"Boston—heard of it, but never been there. Robert is your given name. What is your last name?"

"Isenberg."

"Sounds Jewish. Are you Jewish?"

"Yes, I am. Every day."

"There aren't many Jews up there in Boston, are there?" She turned to Biffy. "Have you ever heard of a Jew from Boston? I thought they were all in New York."

"No, never heard of one from Boston," agreed Biffy, "but I've slept with two Jewish guys."

Lauren smirked. "Were they any good?"

"One was very good. The other talked too much. I did them both a favor. I gave forth with my very best noises and a loud scream at the end. But listen to this. I screamed so loud with the talky-talky guy that he took his hands off of my nubbies and put his fingers in his ears. I'm not sure, but I'm pretty sure, he mumbled, 'What's all the fuss about?' I never saw him again, although he didn't stop calling."

Biffy sighed.

Lauren smiled. "Let's take a bite of this Jewish delivery boy's sandwich, and then send him back to 85th Street."

Then as she chewed vociferously on her sandwich she said, "Yum, fucking, yum delicious! Hey, Biffy, let's tie up Boston and keep him here. He can cook all our meals and once in a while, we can let him pleasure us."

"I've got to get back. I've got a few people waiting for me. Very glad you liked my sandwich. Hope to come again. Just one more thing. You need to pay me, two dollars and fifty-five cents."

Lauren grabbed her pocketbook and handed me three dollars. "I put in a tip. You do take tips, don't you?" she said as she winked at Biffy.

As I began to open the front door, the doorman pulled it open for me.

"And how did you do up there with those two devils?" he asked as he saluted again.

I nodded. "They loved my sandwiches. I can't repeat the words they used to describe them."

The doorman grimaced. "Ahh, and it's a good day when you can please those two. Remember to bring me a sandwich the next time. And it will be nice to see you again. It gets lonely out here."

6

SUE QUESTIONS AND CONFESSES

I HURRIED BACK to my place. I made even better time. I laughed to myself, *less traffic*. There really were fewer people walking.

Jake had the same shit-eating grin, only wider. The three girls were sitting at the table munching on their sandwiches. Jake preened.

"I made everybody, including myself, two sandwiches. Sorry, nothing left for you!" Jake advised.

Donna smiled. "Smashing!"

Every so often her London came sneaking out. She

had come to New York from London when she was fourteen.

She looked British, a little Elizabeth Taylorish . . . dark hair, incredible blue eyes. She was special.

"I mean, really smashing!" Donna repeated.

Sandy echoed Donna, "This is by far the best roast beef sandwich I've ever tasted, as a matter of fact, the best sandwich I've ever had."

Jake and Lois almost in unison asked, "So how was the delivery?"

"You had to be there." I grinned. "Two debs. One named Biffy if you can believe that and the caller was Lauren."

Lois exhaled. "Okay! Let's make believe we were there. Do tell! Do tell."

"Well, they wanted to know where I came from before New York. They were especially intrigued that I was a Jew from Boston. It was almost like they had never heard of Boston, or at least that there were any Jews in Boston."

Lois inquired, "Were they anti-Semitic?"

"No, on the contrary. Biffy mentioned that she had slept with two Jewish guys."

Jake roared, "You got to be shitting us. You go up to their apartment for the first time as a G-D damned delivery boy and they're telling you who they fucked?"

Jake was in total disbelief.

"You had to be there. Biffy complained that one of

the Jewish guys couldn't shut up. He almost messed up her orgasm."

Sandy smiled. "Sounds like a guy I once slept with. He kept asking me how I was doing. I kind of liked it, at least in the beginning."

Lois snickered. "There you go bragging again."

"Actually, the important question is not who shagged whom, but how did they like Robert's roast beef sandwiches?" asked Donna.

I responded, "They loved them, they wanted me to stay and cook for them!"

Jake jumped in, "And you didn't stay, you came back to us. We are so very grateful."

"Well, let me thank you all again for all you did tonight. Let's meet here again tomorrow and make plans."

"I can't," Sandy explained. "I can come by for a little while, but, believe it or not, I have another date with that 'can't-shut-up Jewish guy.' I think he's going to be very rich. He does something in the stock market, but I don't understand exactly what it is. He's also kind of cute, especially when he's not talking. But I'll be back. I want to be part of this great launching."

"I guess we should all leave and let the 'delivery boy' get some rest." Jake was at his sarcastic best.

"Okay, see you tomorrow night at about six. There will be more roast beef and I'll make a salad too."

Off they went.

The place was suddenly quiet. I was about to wash up, when the phone rang.

"It's me, Sue. How did it go? I'm stuck in Chicago, so you won't hear any stomping from me tonight."

"It went well. Jake and the three girls stuffed one hundred pamphlets into mailboxes. I made one delivery to 5th Avenue. It was fun. I delivered three sandwiches to a girl's apartment."

"Wow! That's impressive to get a call for three sandwiches on the very first night. What were the girls like?"

"They were funny. They seemed to care more about where I was from than tasting the sandwiches. They kept saying that I didn't look like a delivery boy. Then when they found out I was Jewish, they really had something going on about me being a Jewish delivery boy."

"Were they pretty?"

"Yup, but don't ask if they had 'big bazookas,' to quote your term. Anyway, I didn't check."

"How did they find out you were Jewish?"

"Well, I told them my last name and they responded with something like 'You must be Jewish.' I told them I was."

"Did they ask you if you had a girlfriend?"

"Hey, I delivered three sandwiches and told them I was Jewish. End of story."

"I'm going to tell you something that we haven't

talked about before."

"Yuh, what's that?"

"You may have guessed, but I haven't had a lot of experience. I was never particularly comfortable around guys. I've only had one boyfriend. I mean a serious one. He and I were high school sweethearts. Besides you, he's the only other guy I've ever slept with. I only slept with him twice. Once when I was leaving for TWA training and a second time when we both came home for Thanksgiving."

"No, I didn't guess. I really didn't think about it. Do you remember what happened that first night? I was so excited looking at you that my penis, or should I call him by his name, 'Mr. Pecker,' while I was unzipping my fly, 'Mr. Pecker' got stuck in the zipper. OUCH!!"

Sue laughed. "You mentioned that. I saw you struggling, but I was much too nice to say anything. I guess you liked what you were looking at. I know everyone says how pretty I am. I wish I thought so."

"Okay, so you are a funny face with small boobs. I call them, as you know, 'little uppies.' And you know I treasure 'little uppies.' Anyway, tell me about your high school sweetie."

"Very different from you and most guys. He was exceptionally nice and very considerate. Unlike you, he didn't have an edge. But I have to admit, I like your edge. I like it enough, so I've made love to you and you are only my second ever."

"You mentioned that earlier. I'm truly honored."

"Don't be so sarcastic. I like your edge, not your chisel."

Sue's voice was sharp.

Then Sue softened as she whispered, "Can you keep a secret? I really couldn't stand my boyfriend being a goody, goody two shoes. Sometimes I wanted to scream, but mostly it made me feel bad about myself and my many shortcomings."

"Hey, this call must be costing a fortune."

"Not a problem. I get all of this free when I get stuck in another city due to a cancellation." Sue sighed. "Besides I missed you. I wanted to hear all about your first delivery day, not so much about your penis getting stuck in your zipper."

"Okay, so you'll be back tomorrow, and I can expect a loud foot stomp. Right?"

"Yup, I'll practice tonight. Only kidding, I don't want to get thrown out of this hotel."

"Oh, by the way, the moaning was very bad last night. She has taken to banging on the wall."

"Damn, we'll have to do something. Wishing you a good night's sleep, so you'll be plenty bushy tailed for me tomorrow evening."

"Can't wait. I'll even get my zipper to stay out of it."

***

The next day, I got into work early again. I wanted more flyers. Wherever I roamed, somebody would yell out, "I hope you didn't poison anyone last night. Ha, ha, ha!!"

Gussie grinned at me. "I knew you'd be back for more. How many this time? You know I can only do so much. If the bosses find out, I'm a dead bunny."

"How's about two hundred for now, that'll last me a good while."

"Okay, but go about your business and come back early tomorrow. I'll have this batch for you."

***

I got home early enough to pick up a three-pound roast beef from Mario, the butcher. I put it right in the oven. It should be roasted in one hour. Jake and the girls would be arriving soon. Jake was the first to arrive.

"So far I'm having fun, but watch out. I'll let you know when this begins to feel like work. By the way I still can't get over Biffy and Lauren. I wish I'd been there."

A few minutes later Lois and Donna arrived. Lois touched her nose.

She exclaimed, "The smell of the roast beef cooking is whetting our appetites!"

Donna breathed deeply. "Let's get the bloody show going here, I'm famished."

Teasing, I tried to encourage them, "When you guys all get back, sandwiches will be waiting!"

Jake called, "Okay, girls, I'm ready to start."

Together, my crew headed out the door.

7

SALADS AND SARDINES

JAKE, DONNA, AND Lois all came back at the same time.

"Now I'm absolutely starving," Donna whimpered. "I thought you were going to make a salad to go along with the roast beef."

"Give me a minute. It won't take but a few minutes. Does anybody want sardines in their salad?" I asked. "Sardines are supposed to be good for you."

"Yuck," said Jake with a grimace, "and I believe I speak for all three of us."

"Wrong!" Donna quipped. "I like the slimy little buggers."

"I can take them or leave them," commented Lois.

To settle it, I declared, "Everything in today's world

is so damn controversial. I'll open a can and put them next to the salad and if you like the 'slimy little buggers,' by all means add them in."

I made the salad and two heaping roast beef sandwiches for everybody. All the food disappeared in very little time, including the sardines. All four of us were patting our happy bellies and saying how delicious it all was.

I began, "We still have one hundred more flyers to stuff in mailboxes, but before we do that, let's set up a new strategy for delivery. Since I believe this delivery idea is just getting started, I'm sure I need to be here to make the sandwiches."

Jake grinned. "Hmm, we'll all talk tomorrow. You still look tired from that delivery, one block away. We'll let you get some much-needed rest."

All three filed out.

I picked up the Jimmy Breslin article I had started to read. Then I heard a foot stomp. I put the newspaper down and practically flew up the stairs.

Sue opened the door with a big smile. "Welcome and please sit down at the table. I put out some wine and cheese."

"Why would you go to all that trouble? I just ate two yummy roast beef sandwiches. I'm full. I know I should have brought you one, but I was in such a hurry to see you, I just ran up the stairs."

Sue murmured, "The reason I went to all that

trouble is I wanted to talk. I have a few questions. I'd love to know more about you."

"Like what? Like what would you like to know?"

"Like why that girl asked if you were Jewish?" Sue asked.

I protested, "I already told you why. She asked my name and it sounds Jewish. She may have thought I look Jewish? Who the hell knows?"

"I'm puzzled about Jews. I never knew any growing up. There were some where I grew up, but they lived in a very different section. My dad always would say, 'Those Jews stick together!' My mom would always add, 'Like glue.' What does it feel like being Jewish, Robert? On Sunday evenings we'd all sit around watching the Colgate Comedy Hour, Martin and Lewis, sometimes Jack Benny. My dad always would say, 'Those Jewish guys all change their last names. Who do they think they are fooling?' My mom would nod knowingly."

I exclaimed, "What does it feel like being whatever the Christ you are!"

"Robert, stop!" Sue snapped, then pleaded, "You know very well being Jewish is different. I'm trying to learn what it's like, because I care so much about you. Is it difficult to be Jewish? Is it more fun or is it no fun? I'm Miss Middle America, aren't I? Real red hair, very white skin, what they would call a real red-blooded American girl? Here I am trying to learn a thing or two from you, since you are my great lover friend. You are not helping."

"I'm sorry, but I can't sum it up in a few words. I myself wonder about it from time to time. I'm puzzled, as you would say. We Jews have had our share of the world's craziness. Many people were and are taught to hate us from childbirth. There is little a sole person like me can do about it, but I eat pork, lobster, bacon, and love sleeping with a Miss Middle American girl with real red hair that looks a little like you."

Sue winked. "I haven't mentioned you to my parents. Anyway, we aren't really dating. So no need. Right?"

"Thank goodness! A few years ago, I was at an all-boys camp. Every other evening, I would meet up on a deserted island between our two camps with this lovely girl, who was at an all-girls camp. It was glorious. It was a time beautifully spent, except for the mosquitoes. I've often wondered what the mosquitoes ate when we weren't there. Anyway, as it happened, she and I entered our freshman year of college at the same school. I could never locate her. It seemed she was avoiding me like a malignant virus. Finally, I did spot her at a coffee shop. I hurried right up to her, 'Why are you ducking me? Was it something I said or did?' She whispered, 'I told my dad about you being Jewish and all. He forbade me to even speak to you again ever.' It was so impersonal, just hate ridden."

"Really impersonal?" asked Sue.

"Maybe both personal and impersonal, but even though I was only seventeen, I wasn't surprised. I had run into so much of it at Boys Latin School and then the Army. I wondered if I was a particular target because I'm short." "Okay, enough Jewish talk for one night. Let's get back to checking on my little pink nipples. I must tell you that they aren't Kosher either."

I smiled and nodded.

***

Jake and I met the following night, without the girls who had been doing the stuffing.

Jake suggested, "Every other night, let each of us take turns either making the deliveries or making the roast beef. If we need more help, I've got all the girl's numbers. By the way, I want to introduce you to Ira. Ira Landess is a buddy of mine from Brandeis. I'll check to see if he's available Sunday for lunch."

Jake picked up the phone and called Ira.

Jake turned towards me while still on the phone. "Ira would love to meet us for lunch at one of his favorite restaurants. You will really like Ira a lot. He's a native New Yorker. Sometimes it seems like he knows everybody. Another thing about Ira, he's almost as good as I am at choosing great places to eat. He wants to meet us at a Chinese restaurant called Shanghai. I've been there with Ira. It's a winner. Good food, great prices! I'm endorsing it! It's on upper Broadway near Columbia. Almost all the patrons are Chinese."

Jake gave me a thumbs up.

After Jake left, Pat called. "I'm starting to go out with Jacoby. He's so much fun and so bright. I thought I'd let you know. I thought it was only fair to tell you. I also know how competitive you are. I suggest you let it rest."

I hung up the phone without speaking a word. I was furious with myself for not breaking it off. *Why hadn't I been more honest with Pat? Why was I such a coward?*

At least she was being truthful. *Get over it. Pat is a thousand miles away. It could be a million miles. No matter. Consider yourself lucky. You had a great summer. Now get over yourself and Pat. There are new worlds to conquer. Roast beef sandwiches to deliver. So shut the fuck up!* However, I did vow that no matter what, I would never speak to her again.

8

GETTING TO MEET IRA

JAKE AND I grabbed a taxi to 102nd Street and Broadway. As we exited the cab, there were the Chinese and American huge glittering letters welcoming us to the Shanghai restaurant. Below the Shanghai sign there were letters, VERY GOOD FOOD. I was hungry already.

Jake and I walked in and were immediately welcomed by a rather chubby, smiling hostess. She pointed to a table.

"Come in. Let me sit you down."

Jake responded, "We are meeting our friend. We'll take a look around."

We didn't have to look around. It was incredibly easy to spot Ira. Everybody else was Chinese. Ira spotted us and stood up with a big welcoming smile brightening his face.

When we reached the table, Ira and Jake embraced as if they hadn't seen each other in years. I had never seen two guys hug like that in Dorchester. I thought if they had, they'd have been arrested. Finally they let go.

Ira looked at me and looked over at Jake. "Yankel, who have you brought with you?"

Then Ira broke into a big grin. "Robert, you are Robert, right? I've heard all about you. You and Yankel come from the same area in Boston, but you hardly knew each other there. Now you two have decided to be buddies. New York City will do that to you. You need all the friends you can get here. Right, Yankel?"

Ira laughed.

"Yes, we grew up a few streets from each other, but had never spent much time together. Even so, Jake was kind enough to let me stay at his place when I arrived in the city. It gave me time to find a place of my own. We've had a lot of fun since!"

Jake murmured, "That's your side of the story."

It wasn't long into our conversation that I knew I was going to like Ira a lot. I was impressed by everything he had to say. Ira was a high school teacher. He chose the most difficult areas in NYC to teach in. He felt that he learned so much from the kids he was teaching, he thought that he should be paying them. It seemed Ira knew everybody. He had writer friends. One of them had just published a book. Hollywood was calling his writer buddy daily. Best of all, Ira had grown up on the same street as Art Garfunkel and Paul Simon and they were good friends. Ira put his hand in his pocket and took out six tickets. He spread the tickets out on the table.

"Listen here. Simon and Garfunkel are going to be the opening act for the Mamas and Papas next Sunday at Forest Hills. I've got six great seats. Does anyone want them?"

"Wow! Wow! Wow!" Jake and I responded together.

Not knowing what to say, I asked, "What do we order here?"

"Yankel, I know you are not easy when it comes to food. Do you remember if you liked anything the last time we came here ?"

"Hey, before you guys order . . . yes, I'd love to go and have two tickets. Is that okay with you, Ira? As far as the food goes, you guys order, I know it will be fine with me."

"Okay, I'd love you to be my guest. Who will you be taking? Yankel told me you were playing house with some girl from the University of Michigan who has large breasts. I love big tits. I know it makes me sound obnoxious, but fuck it! That's who I am. Will you be bringing her? I believe Yankel told me her name was Pat."

"Yes, her name was Pat, but nope." I clarified, "I hope to bring Sue. She lives in the same building as I do. Pat and I broke up."

Jake snickered. "Sue lives directly over Robert and they have a deal."

Ira protested, "Wait a minute. I'm not going to get to see Pat with the big balloons. Give me back those tickets!"

Ira laughed and waved at me.

"Only kidding, Robert. I really look forward to meeting Sue. What does she do, besides live over you?"

"She's a flight attendant for TWA. She has only been in New York for a short time. Sue is from the Midwest. Like me, Sue is trying to get a grasp of the city."

"Will she be able to get time off? And what does Yankel here mean that you two have a deal?"

"Yeah, she can get time off if she puts in for it far enough ahead. I know she'll be very excited. She loves both groups. As far as the deal goes, when Sue comes back from a flight and she's not too tired, she stomps on the floor, which means I'm to come right up."

Ira screamed, "Wait a fucking minute here. You're shitting me! No date! No going out anywhere! No fucking food! No drinks!! You've got to be kidding me! You come all the way from Boston, to tell me this. First big tits! Now this bullshit stomping story! What the fuck do you have going for you? I'm ordering the food, before I shit my pants!"

Ira called the waiter over. The waiter seemed to know Ira. They smiled and laughed a lot as they peered over the crinkled menu. Ira pointed a lot at the menu and at Jake. The waiter smiled as he checked out Jake. He nodded at Ira and finally left with his notes.

The food was delicious, although I had no idea what it was. We split the very inexpensive bill three ways. Because of his generosity with the tickets and his savvy, Jake and I tried to wrestle the bill away from Ira. Ira would have none of it.

As Ira got into a taxi, he yelled at me from the half-closed window, "Could you call Pat and ask her to forgive you for whatever the hell you did and get her back here?" He hollered as the cab screeched away, "I want to check out those tits! Damn!"

Jake and I talked on the cab ride back. We planned who would slice and who would deliver on which days during the following week. Jake and I wished each other a good night.

As Jake shuffled off, he added, "Can't wait for next Sunday!"

I called Sue as soon as I got to my apartment. "Just got back. You aren't going to believe this. I met this guy Ira who grew up with Simon and Garfunkel. He gave Jake and me tickets to their concert next Sunday in Forest Hills. See if you can get the day off. The Mamas and Papas will be there too. I don't deliver on Sundays, so not a problem for me."

Sue cried out, "I'll be there if I have to steal one of

TWA's planes! Hey, by the way, it's early. Come on up. I'm feeling very down. I've been listening to that crazy woman scream all day. By the way, do you happen to have any of those Fairly Famous's Roast Beef sandwiches that you might bring up to me?"

"I'm on my way, and this time with a thick and juicy sandwich, if you get my meaning?"

Sue laughed. "I do. Hurry before it spills over, if you get my meaning?"

Sue was waiting at the door with her hands reaching for the sandwich. Even before she took a bite she exclaimed, "Yum!"

Sue began to munch on the sandwich. She pointed for me to sit down on one of her cushy chairs.

"How were your deliveries last week?"

"Not bad. They're getting better each week. Each evening, there are more and more deliveries."

Sue smiled. "You know this could turn into something big, speaking of hot and juicy."

I laughed. "Glad you like what I'm delivering."

"Anything to take my mind off that crazy woman." Sue looked at me. "Only kidding. Speaking of taking my mind off of certain things, please stay here tonight. Maybe we can drown out her noise."

"You twisted my arm again. But I'd prefer a pretty please."

I began to unbutton my shirt. Sue was laughing. Her blue eyes were twinkling as we held each other.

***

The following Sunday we all met at my apartment. Jake was with Diane Bishop. Diane and Jake both worked at Fairchild Press as copy editors. Jake had mentioned Diane to me before. She was from Lowell, Mass. She had come to New York to go to Barnard. Jake had stated that she was very smart and that she loved movies and knew a lot about them. Jake also mentioned that Diane could be very moody. Diane was best friends with some girl named Ellen that Jake was lusting after.

Ira was with Doreen Rappaport, his very long-time girlfriend from Brandeis. I shook Doreen's hand. "Great to meet you."

Doreen smiled a very wide smile and enthused, "Same here!"

She was almost Ira's height and quite attractive in a very wholesome way. I liked her immediately, as I had Ira. She motioned for me to come a little closer.

Doreen confided to me, "Ira and I are going straight to Artie's house before the concert. Artie's mother, and his brother Jules have asked us to come for a pre-concert celebration. His Mom is serving up her extra special chicken soup. It was made with ginger for strength and luck. She was saying that she couldn't count the times that she'd gone by that concert stadium, and now her son Artie will be performing there in front of thousands of screaming fans. We will have to leave now."

9

THE SIMON AND GARFUNKEL CONCERT

I TEASED JAKE, "Aren't you going to introduce me to your very pretty friend here?"

Diane reached out to me and smiled. "I'm Diane Bishop. Jake and I work together at Fairchild Press. I'm so excited about going tonight. I can't wait to get there. How about you? Are you a fan of either of these groups?"

"Nice to meet you. Very glad Jake and you were able to make it. Yuh, I like both groups. Paul Simon sure can write, and so can John Phillips. Let's leave now and get our seats as soon as possible. Who knows who might try to grab our seats if we don't hurry? We're talking Queens."

The four of us grabbed a cab after about a ten-minute wait. Diane jumped into the front seat. Sue was practically trembling.

"This would never have happened in Topeka!" I chuckled. "Or Dorchester either."

We got to our seats before there were any other people around. Sue sat on my right. Diane and Jake sat on my left. Ira and Doreen had their seats a few rows away. We were in the third row. They were right up front. Diane leaned towards me. "I heard from Jake that you're from Dorchester, the same as Jake. I'm from Lowell."

"I've never been to Lowell. What's it like?" I asked.

"You don't want to know or go," Diane murmured.

"What brought you to the city?" I asked.

"Barnard." Diane smiled. "Barnard, Barnard, and Barnard! What brought you here? Jake told me you two are making and delivering roast beef sandwiches. Surely you didn't move to New York City to deliver roast beef sandwiches?"

"Not exactly," I said nodding. "But you see, I hate my job. I wanted to create a business with few start-up costs. I looked around the neighborhood. I saw a lot of young single people scurrying around. They all looked hungry. I thought what they need is to be fed and what better way than my juicy sandwiches?"

Diane laughed. "I hate my job too and Jake hates his. Jake and I are coffee break buddies. We both get a chance every morning to rant to each other over our bagels. You say that you have never been to Lowell. Well, I've never been to Dorchester. It sounds like since both of us have come from the Boston area and that both of us hate our jobs, it's possible we could have coffee and some laughs. I promise not to rant. Here's my number and address. If you get a chance, give me a call."

Diane handed me a piece of paper with her address and phone number scribbled on it.

Sue, who had been staring at the empty stage, turned to me and frowned. "What are you two talking about?"

"Diane is from the Boston area too and we were just comparing notes," I explained.

Sue practically screamed, "Only a few more minutes before Simon and Garfunkel will be out there!"

She was almost right. At first, Simon appeared by himself. He began doing a Lenny Bruce type monologue. I was startled. We all had come for the music. What was up? He was actually funny in a very dark, acerbic sort of way, but what's going on here, I wondered? Was Garfunkel sick? Perhaps the soup didn't work?

Sue elbowed me again. "I'm so nervous. What do

you think is happening?"

"No idea."

I held Sue's wrist. It seemed to calm her.

I glanced over at Diane and Jake. They were busy quietly chatting and seemed totally unconcerned. A few minutes later, Art Garfunkel sauntered out. He was tall and handsome. He was almost pretty. He had long curly blond hair. He probably looked even taller than he actually was, because Paul Simon was actually rather short. Garfunkel approached Simon and put his arm around Paul, as if to say everything was all right.

They quickly broke into *The Sound of Silence*. They didn't stop singing for the next fifty-five minutes until they concluded with *He Was My Brother*. There was a binding stillness. Then came the big smiles and warm waves to us, the audience. We broke enthusiastically into applause. There was a brief interim. Someone, who evidently worked for the producers of the show, told us how glad they all were that we had come for this amazing show. He announced, "The good news is the Mamas and Papas will be out here in a few minutes. The bad news is Michelle Phillips will not be joining them. Michelle is not feeling well tonight."

John Phillips walked on. "We are going to treat you to something we haven't done for anyone else. We are going to sing all of the songs that we have just recorded on our newest unreleased album and finish up with *California Dreaming*. We know you have all been waiting to hear that. Too bad we won't be going back to LA just yet. Thanks to you all for being so patient and forgiving us for Michelle's absence."

Ira turned to us and grinned. "I know why Michelle didn't show. I'll tell you guys later. Let's all meet at Robert's apartment after the show."

The Mamas and Papas did just what John Phillips promised. They sang songs we had never heard before. Then they brought the house down with *California Dreaming.*

I announced to Sue, still holding her wrist, "I'll have to tell Ira that we sure got our money's worth. It was truly spectacular!"

Sue moved closer to me. "They are so creative. Mama Cass was awesome, I hardly missed Michelle Phillips."

I muttered, "Maybe you didn't, but I did. I wouldn't care if she sang or not. I just wanted to see her up close from these amazing seats. She's some beauty."

"Too bad." Sue smiled. "You guys, always leering and having those stupid, unrealistic fantasies that don't do you any good. I'd suggest not just you, but all guys, should try to grow up."

Diane had been chatting with Jake. She turned her head to me. "Did you love it?"

"I did. It was every bit as good as I expected and then some, but I did miss Michelle."

"I overheard Sue and I strongly second it." Diane

grinned.

We grabbed a taxi. The driver agreed to take us all back to my place. We were jammed in. Doreen and Ira somehow managed to get in the front seat. Doreen was practically sitting on Ira's lap. The rest of us crammed into the back seat. I had both women pressing against me. I was not unhappy.

As soon as we arrived at my apartment, Jake announced that he didn't know about the rest of us, but he was starving and that he didn't want another roast beef sandwich.
Ira protested, "Doreen and I have just heard about them. We've never tasted one."
"Yeah," uttered Doreen, "Jake had my mouth watering when he described them."
Diane exclaimed, "Neither have I. I'll have Jake bring me one for lunch one day, if that's okay with you, Robert."
"Sorry guys, it's Sunday. We sold out on Saturday. I don't have enough left for even half a sandwich. Call me during the week and we'll make them up special for all of you. I promise."
Ira agreed, "Okay. Who needs roast beef when we can pick up one of New York City's best pizzas on 86th and 1st? It's called Sal's."
Jake countered, "You think their pizza is one of the

best? Have you tried Lucia's—it's on 3rd? No frigging comparison. I'm surprised at you. But I'm so hungry and your place is closer, so I'll go along with you. Let's call up for three large pizzas."

"Is everybody happy with tomato, cheese, and bacon?" yelled Ira.

Jake commented, "It's not a Jewish thing. But I just don't like bacon. How about one with only tomato and cheese?"

Doreen smiled. "Anything to please you, Jake, but let Ira tell you the juiciest gossip as to why Michelle Phillips didn't show."

Ira lowered his voice, almost as if someone outside my apartment could hear.

"Michelle was caught sleeping, or should I say fucking, Denny, the other Papa. Michelle Phillips is married to John Phillips. Evidently they were not even discreet."

I smirked. "Wow! I guess Denny had something to sing about."

"That's not all," Ira continued. "Mama Cass has always been in love with Denny. She thought he was in love with her. Evidently Cass attacked Michelle, saying. 'You are so very beautiful. You could have any guy. Why did you have to take Denny away from me?' John was furious. He decided to ban Michelle from the group for an unspecified time. As far as Simon and Garfunkel and Artie coming out late, something was going on between those two. I guess we'll find out in due time."

The pizza arrived and was devoured in minutes. We all parted, except Sue.

Sue grinned. "What a great night. I liked everybody and everything, even the pizza. It was delicious. Who would have thought two weeks ago that we'd be going to such a concert? I'm very tired though. I hope that crazy lady won't be screaming tonight. Now listen good! I'll probably have my stomping shoes on tomorrow evening." Sue smiled, as she softly closed the door behind her.

***

The next evening, I sliced and Jake delivered. It was somewhat quiet. We only delivered six sandwiches. The following night around 7:00, Jake picked up the phone and began writing. His hands were shaking. He hung up the phone.

"You had better sit down. Some place called Lloyd's just called and they want fifty sandwiches now!"

"What!" I cried. "Where are we going to get fifty frigging sandwiches? Where exactly is Lloyd's located?"

Jake exclaimed, "Their address is right around the corner! They're on 1st and 91st. They told me they are on the northwest corner. What the hell are we going to do? I'll bet we don't have enough meat for twenty sandwiches and the butcher is closed up tight!"

I very lightly poked Jake in the stomach. "You know what? Let's make up what we have. Let's deliver it. We'll go see what's going on at Lloyd's. I've noticed that place. I just didn't know the exact address. I even told Pat that you and I had drinks there when she had called and I hadn't answered. Actually, I had been upstairs with Sue. Lloyd's looks very crowded and very noisy. Definitely a happening spot."

10
LLOYD'S

JAKE AND I walked across 1st Avenue, to the swinging doors that would let us into the bar. As we entered, we were astonished by the crowd. Everyone looked my age and as if they belonged It seemed everybody was speaking at once. The noise was deafening.

"Hey, are you Fairly Famous?" yelled the bartender, smiling at us, showing off gaps among his teeth. "Did you bring the roast beef sandwiches we ordered?"

"Yes, I'm Robert and this is Jake. We did the best we could, but we could only muster up eighteen sandwiches. Next time, give us some notice and we'll get you as many as you want."

"Okay, for now. I get it. But our problem is we don't

know how many people are coming. We don't RSVP." He laughed. "By the way my name is Charlie. I'm the manager and sometimes bartender here."

"I see you have a nice kitchen in the back. Where's your cook?"

Charlie frowned. "We've had a ton of cooks; they don't stay long."

"You are looking at two. Right in front of you."
"When can you start?" yelled Charlie.

"Yesterday! But seriously, we have to make some arrangements. It won't take long. How is next Monday?"

Charlie was receptive. "Great! I'll be really looking forward to Monday. I'll tell Gloria. She owns the place. Let's you and Jake go back in the kitchen with me and we will work out the details."

Jake and I followed Charlie into the kitchen. There was a good size refrigerator with a freezer. A slicing machine on the kitchen counter seemed to be just waiting for us to come and use it. The stove looked more than ample. There were plenty of knives, forks, and spoons in a drawer under the counter. Charlie noticed my pleased expression.

"We should have everything you need in order to serve sandwiches. If we don't, ask me, I'll do my best to help. How would you like to work this out? I'm talking about money. Let me tell you a little secret: according to state law, we are required to serve food if we serve alcohol. Hopefully we will be serving a lot of liquor and

I'm thinking your sandwiches should make them very thirsty. So what I'm saying is you keep the money from all your sales, and we'll keep the money from all of ours."

"Sounds good. I'm also offering to provide your staff with free food should they ask."

"I like it." Charlie nodded. "I'll throw in free drinks for you guys, or anyone else you might have working the kitchen."

All three of us shook hands. Charlie went back to the bar.

I turned towards Jake. "What do you think?"

Jake grinned. "I believe you've found gold, but I'll still have my job so I won't be as available as you."

"Okay, I'll work almost every evening. You work Sundays and give me the day off. Whatever money you take in on Sundays, you keep."

"Deal," Jake confirmed, "and if you need a night off let me know."

Charlie paid us for the sandwiches.

I went back to my place and so did Jake. Sue had tomorrow off and wanted me to call if I got home at a reasonable hour. I called her.

"Sue, what's up? I can't wait to tell you what happened tonight."

"C'mon up, I can't wait to hear. Hope it's good news."

I flew up the steps. Sue had already opened the

door. Her arms stretched out to hug me.

"So? What's the big news? What can't you wait to tell me?"

"Well! We got a call for fifty sandwiches tonight."

"What! What? From where?"

"Lloyd's, the bar just down the street, and they took Jake and me in as their cooks!"

"Wait a second here. You are going too fast. How on earth did you deliver that many sandwiches?"

"We didn't. We brought them what we had, which were eighteen sandwiches. But the best part is they have a good sized, well-equipped kitchen, and we've been hired to provide the restaurant with food. We also made a deal. Free drinks for Jake and me and we'll provide their people with free food."

Sue pondered before she spoke, "I don't like bars. I don't like free drinks. But I do like the idea of serving a lot of people sandwiches. You know you can't just serve sandwiches. You'll need something to go along with them."

"Yup," I agreed. "There is a deli near where I work that has the best potato salad and coleslaw I've ever tasted. I'll also make salads with lettuce and cherry tomatoes. But what have you got against bars and free drinks?"

"Bars are the worst places ever created. They stink! They stink of smoke and booze. I hate them. Just walking into one, I walk out feeling dirty. So, while I'm happy for you that you have a location that could bolster your business, I'm not happy for us. And besides, I'm in a feisty mood. I tried to get some much-needed rest and that crazy woman didn't stop screaming."

"Wow! Very sorry you didn't get any sleep, but even more upset that you hate the deal Jake and I made."

"Robert, you are my very best friend. Let me think it over. I'll check out Lloyd's, maybe I won't hate it as much as every other bar I've ever set foot in."

"If you hate bars so much, why have you ever gone to more than one?"

"Two reasons! I've told you that I get asked out to dinner a lot by passengers. Usually they take me to fancy pancy restaurants and you have to get by the bar to dine. Whoever is sitting there drinking when I rush by is still sitting there drinking when I leave. I ask myself, 'Don't they have anywhere better to go?' Sometimes I ask the guy I'm with. The other reason is that whenever my fellow stewardesses want to celebrate, it's always at some bar. I usually decline, but they are persistent and insist that I come.

"As soon as I enter one of those smoke-filled, stinky places, because I'm tired, I usually make the mistake of sitting down on a bar stool. I've been on my feet all day. Not two seconds goes by, when some creepy guy comes over, places his hand on my arm and says, 'Do you come here often?' I reply, 'NO! And I don't intend to come back!' Next they usually say, 'Do you know how beautiful you are?' My reply to that is, 'Yes, which makes me far too good for you, so go talk to someone else!' I've even added, 'Besides I have a boyfriend. I think he would mind.'"

"Got it." I grinned. "You just don't like being asked questions. Right? Anyway, I thought you'd be excited about Lloyd's. I'll ask one more question. How would you like me to kiss that beautiful body of yours from head to toe?"

"I am very excited for you. I'm just worried about what will happen to us. I love our friendship. I love it that you are right under me and are able to come up here to be with me when I'm home. Call me selfish. I hate to lose even one drop of that. And as far as the kisses from head to toe, I told you I was feisty tonight, so please, pretty please start at my feet."

"Your wish is granted. Feet first," I replied.

11

ABBIE HOFFMAN OFFERS

ME MY FIRST JOINT

I HAD A lot to do the next morning. I had to get to work early. I needed menus. I'd have to plead with Gussie, one last time. How many would I need? I'll ask for seventy-five and accept her probable offer of fifty. I'll need to sketch it out and decide on prices. No problem. I'll charge the same eighty-five cents for the sandwich and forty-five cents for all salads.

I arrived at work very early. Gussie was already there.

"And what can I do for you now, Mr. Big Business-

Man?"

"Hey, Gussie, I've got exciting news."

"Yeah, like what?" asked Gussie. "Somehow I don't think this will be exciting for me."

"Last night I made a deal with a local bar to serve food to their customers. I'm going to need menus. Here, I sketched it all out for you."

"Oh, thanks very much. You sketched the menu out for me and you expect me to run off copies for you. Hey, Mr. Big Shot, I suspect you will be leaving us very shortly. What's in it for me? You haven't even brought me one sandwich. Look, we are both lucky the bosses don't come back here. How many do you want?"

"Seventy-five," I whispered.

Gussie winked. "I'll run off forty for you, and don't come back here without a couple of those roast beef sandwiches."

"Okay, I'll bring a couple tomorrow. Thanks again. You have been a very good friend."

Gussie growled, "Friend schmend, get out of my sight. Those sandwiches had better be good. I'll have the menus ready for you tomorrow."

At lunch, I went to the Jewish deli that served the amazing potato salad and coleslaw. I sought out Manny, who almost always waited on me.

"I have a question for you."

"Yeah, and what's the big question?" asked Manny.

"How is it that your guys in the kitchen always make the potato salad and coleslaw so good and always exactly the same taste?"

"Schmuck!" Manny hollered. "We don't have any guys back in the kitchen. We don't even really have a kitchen. I have a question for you. How come all you Boston guys are so stupid? You have all those fancy colleges up there, but you don't know nothing. Those salads come from a salad manufacturer on the north side of the Bronx. Why? What's it to you?"

"I just made a deal to supply food for a bar in Manhattan. I wanted some salads to go along with my roast beef sandwiches. Your salads are the best."

"Hey, Mr. Schlimiel from Boston, come over here. I'm going to write down the address. See Bill O'Hare. He's the manager. Tell him Manny sent you. Can you remember, Mr. Schlimiel, to keep your mouth shut about what I just gave you? Can you? You'd better, if you know what's good for you or for any girlfriends you might have!"

"Thanks. I'll zip over there right now. Good thing I don't have any girlfriends."

Manny laughed. "Yuh, I'll bet. Who would go out with a funny looking Mr. Schlimiel from Boston?"

"You'd be surprised! I know I am," I replied.

I was off without lunch hoping I'd find the place in no time. I followed the directions Manny had written down and pulled up to a large building that matched the address Manny had handed me. I pulled open the very heavy door and was astonished to see the longest cutting board I'd ever seen, maybe the size of a football field. Puerto Rican men and women were on either side, cutting up cabbage and stuffing it into a very noisy machine. I headed past the cutting board toward the front of the room where I saw a sign with OFFICE printed in capital letters. Behind the desk was a red-faced, stout, but very strong-looking guy. He looked a bit grim. He got up and extended his hand.

"I'm Bill O'Hare, you must be Robert. I just hung up from Manny. He called to tell me you'd be here. He informed me you were a nice Jewish kid from Boston. He also added you don't know shit from Shinola. Well, do you?"

"I know shit when I see it, but don't know much about Shinola. Did he tell you that next week, I'd be starting to serve food in a Manhattan bar?"

"No, he just indicated you were interested in buying our salads."

"I am very much so. What do you charge per pound? Do you deliver?"

"If you can buy five pounds, I'll give you the same price we charge Manny's deli. That would be fifteen cents per pound and usually we will deliver no less than five pounds."

He paused. Then he gave me a long look. *I tried to*

look cool.

"Well, in your case since you are just starting out, we'll let you order three pounds for a while. We like to see young guys like yourself get started. Who knows what it will lead to?"

Bill said in a growl, "But a word to the wise and to the stupid . . . restaurants are not an easy business. You got to know what you are doing at all times. You really have to know shit from Shinola to make a buck in the food business."

I extended my hand. "I know I've got a lot to learn, especially about Shinola."

We both smiled and shook hands. Bill gave me his card. I wrote down my phone number and Lloyd's address.

After work, I'd bring Mario my meat supplier into the loop. I'd also go back to Lloyd's and try to get a clearer lay of the land. I hadn't counted the tables. I hadn't checked how many stools were at the bar. I had a lot to do as well as a lot to learn.

I needed to call my answering service and have them tell anyone who might call that starting Monday, the very same sandwich could be found at Lloyd's at the corner of 91st and 1st.

***

By Sunday I was exhilarated and exhausted. I was going to just try to relax. I put on the exhibition football game—it was the Giants and Philadelphia. The phone rang. It was Ira.

"Whatcha doing? I'd like to come over and introduce you to a friend from Brandeis. Would that be okay?"

"Great. See you soon."

I poured myself a vodka and soda with a touch of cranberry juice and sat back and waited.

The doorbell rang and I buzzed them in. Ira came flying through the door saying, "I'm a big Giant's fan, how are they doing? By the way, this is my buddy from Brandeis. Abbie, Abbie Hoffman, I want you to meet Robert 'Fairly Famous' Isenberg."

I took a look at Abbie. I couldn't believe any white man could have such curly hair.

I had read a little about Abbie in the Village Voice. I didn't know he and Ira were friends. There was something electric about Abbie. I was immediately struck by his charisma and his smile seemed to light up the room.

Abbie looked at me and pointed at my drink. "What's that shit you have there?'

"It's a vodka tonic with a touch of cranberry juice."

"Here, throw that crap out. It will kill you. Try this." He handed me my first toke. Abbie grinned.

"I'll show you what to do with it. You'll love me forever."

He took a puff, held it and then blew the smoke out.

He followed up with even a bigger grin.

I took the toke that Abbie passed back to me. With

a shaking hand, I placed it in my mouth and tried to copy what I had just seen Abbie do. I began to cough violently.

Abbie looked at Ira and laughed.

"It is never easy trying to teach beginners especially if they're from Boston."

Ira looked back at Abbie and asked, "What are you doing to my friend Robert? Anyway, I just spoke to Jake and he tells me that he and Robert are going to supply food for Lloyd's. Lloyd's is that bar we just passed on our way here."

"What kind of food?" asked Abbie.

"Mostly roast beef sandwiches and salads."

"If you had gone to Brandeis with us, you'd be making pastrami sandwiches served with a half sour pickle," Abbie teased. "Anyway, you can count on Ira and me to visit you a lot there. As soon as you settle in, we'll come over. You'll need a following and I'm getting pretty famous. I'm not just fairly famous," Abbie declared.

"Many thanks. I'm starting tomorrow. I think I'll take a run over there later today. I need to check how many tables and how many bar stools they have. Just get a feel for the place. I've never done anything like this before."

"I'm looking forward to that pastrami sandwich, oops I mean roast beef sandwich." Abbie grinned again.

"Me too!" Ira nodded.

"How is your head?" asked Abbie. "I'm guessing this was the first time you tried a joint. If you are planning to have sex soon, you'll need another. I'm leaving it on your television. Try it with your girl. I guarantee, both of you will be screaming. Ira clued me in on your stomping deal. Not bad! But and this is a big 'But,' I'm not a believer in one lady friend. Ira told me you came from Boston. I come from Worcester and I know very well about the great pussy drought up there. But it's very different here in New York City. You should have your pick, especially in a bar and especially serving food. Women love guys who feed them, almost as much as guys who make them laugh."

Ira chimed in, "What if they don't get off like you say, what is your guarantee worth? You remember you gave me and Doreen the same guarantee and neither of us screamed. Maybe a little louder murmur than usual. We never found out what the guarantee was."

"The guarantee is, if you don't get my promised results, I'll come over and do it for you, and I'll do it for Robert here too! On that generous note, I have to leave and meet Jerry. Jerry Rubin, my partner. We are going to try to turn this country upside down. And my new friend Robert has to check the bar out."

"I'll pack it in as well. I'll ask Doreen what she thinks of the guarantee," Ira snickered.

12

LEARNING ABOUT BARS

AFTER IRA AND Abbie left, I needed time to just sit. The joint had made me a little dizzy. I wasn't sure but it seemed that the combination of pot and alcohol were causing me to feel a trifle weak. My goal was to rest a few minutes and then check out Lloyd's. I wanted to see what it would be like on a Sunday.

I walked across the street and made it pretty quickly to 1st Avenue. I knew I was going to be doing this a lot. I decided to time it, just to see how long it would take me to get there from my apartment. When I arrived at the swinging doors, I checked my watch. Nine minutes was all it took.
I walked in. The jukebox was playing *California*

Dreaming by the Mamas and Papas. I wondered if Michelle Phillips was included in this version. I headed right for the kitchen, where I could assess the place. The bar had twelve stools. There were eight facing the bar and two on either end. I noted that there were six people on the stools. They all seemed to be talking at once. I went over to them. One of them got up and greeted me.

"My name is Skip, and this is my friend Dick. Those other two gentlemen are regulars, pretty much like Dick and me. The guy closest to me teaches at NYU. His name is Ernest. He loves to come here and talk politics with the guy sitting next to him. The other guy is Phil. He's an artist who has an opinion on everything. Those two will argue sometimes to closing time, when the bartender has to throw them out. Dick and I don't give a rat's ass about politics. We come here to get a little drunk and check out the girls that frequent the place. Our hope is to get more than a little lucky."

Dick was leaning over and listening with a huge smile on his face. It was one of those ear-to-ear smiles that had you liking him instantly and smiling back at him.

"You must be Robert's Fairly Famous. We saw you head for the kitchen. We heard from Charlie you were going to start serving food this coming Monday. Is that true?"

"Yup, I'm starting Monday. My friend Jake will be in the kitchen on future Sundays. We are excited to be here. I see there are eight tables. Do they fill up much?"

"Yeah, they do. Mostly the girls who come here sit at the tables. We generally sit at the bar," Dick confided. "We were here the night you and Charlie went back in the kitchen. Charlie told us later you made a deal and that you would be serving food. Gloria owns the place. Charlie keeps her happy, if you know what I mean. Charlie can be very charming, and he can be not so charming. He's an alcoholic. Mostly he doesn't drink, but when he does, we've heard he puts on a Gestapo uniform. Both Skip and I wish you only the best. The food here has been iffy. Mostly popcorn or potato chips have been the nightly specials. The cooks Charlie hired usually lasted less than a week. One other thing is a lot of the young lovelies have crushes on Charlie. Gloria doesn't show up that often, so when Charlie is on, he does very well."

"Wow, that's a lot to take in. I hope I can just go about the business of serving food and stay out of the politics. But I do have an aversion to Gestapo uniforms. I'm speaking for most of us Jewish guys. Anyway, it's great to meet you both. Who is the bartender today? When I came in, I caught the back of somebody leaving the bar and heading to the toilet."

"That's George. He bartends Sundays and once in a while during the week. He's about fifty something. Quite distinguished looking. But he has this quirk. When he goes to the toilet, it's forever. Somebody once timed him at thirty-four minutes. Every regular knows, if George goes to the toilet, hold your water for at least an hour. One time a stranger, not knowing , walked in right after George. About a minute or two later, he staggered out. He was coughing and sneezing as he ran out of here. One other thing about George is that he has a very young girlfriend. She usually sits at the bar just staring at George. She didn't show today. Too bad, she's good to look at. She usually gives us a lot of leg."

Skip snickered and added, "Bars are special. Most places are somewhat crazy, but my guess is bars are crazier for obvious reasons. Bars take on personalities just like people. And like-minded people visit like-minded bars. In a way they are family, especially when you are away from home. But the big difference is we get to choose them, or maybe I should say they choose us."

Dick offered, "The other bars, or maybe they consider themselves to be restaurants, like Elaine's, well, their staff visit Lloyd's a lot. They're always bragging about their patrons. Elaine's, for some reason, attracts famous writers and some soon to be famous."

"Like who?" I asked.

"Like Bruce Jay Friedman, Tom Wolfe, Pete Hamill, Jimmy Breslin, Gloria Steinem, Nora Ephron, etc., etc. Need I go on?"

"Do those writers ever come here?"

Skip chimed in, "Nope! We hear the food at Elaine's is really good. The food here has sucked. We don't care about special food. We care about the booze and the young ladies. Besides we hear her food is not cheap."

Dick was nodding. "I don't worry about my stomach, but I do worry about my shlong. Skip didn't mention that we get a group from Malachy's almost every night just before closing. They usually have had more than any human being should have to drink, but they're just getting started. Frank McCourt owns Malachy's. Evidently Malachy is his brother's name. It was also his father's name. Malachy's is a very popular watering hole. It's rough and tumble. We never go there."

"I'm getting the picture. I can only hope that everybody who comes here is very hungry."

Skip smiled and turned to Dick. "Hey, you cheap bastard, Fairly Famous has been listening to our B.S. for way too long. How about you buying him a drink?"

"It would be my pleasure. Robert, what can I get for you?" Dick asked. "George will hopefully be back soon."

"Thanks, guys. Thanks for the offer, and many thanks for all the info. I've got to get back to my place and take care of a few things."

Both Skip and Dick got up and hugged me, saying, "Great to meet you. Our best wishes to Mr. Fairly Famous and our undernourished stomachs."

I timed it on my way home. It was a little over eight minutes. I wondered if it were less time, because maybe

Sue was back. I called her as soon as I got home.

She picked up right away, and hearing my voice began exclaiming, "Where have you been? Don't you know today is Sunday? You should be resting. My foot got tired from stomping. Anyway, come on up and lay your day on me."

I hustled up the stairs. Sue had the door open.

I began, "First, it's great to see you. Second, I had an exciting day. You remember Ira, don't you?"

"Of course! Ira hosted the tickets for the Simon and Garfunkel concert. I liked him a lot and his girlfriend Doreen."

"Well, Ira brought his Brandeis buddy Abbie Hoffman over to meet me. I wish you had been here. I just spent a short time with Abbie, and it seemed as if I knew him forever."

"Why?" Sue pondered. "What made it so special?"

"I'm not sure I can explain it. You have to meet him to get it. He took over as soon as he came in. First, he insulted the drink I was enjoying. He then handed me my first joint. He showed me what to do with it, by lighting up one for himself. I didn't like it much, but I did like Abbie."

"I've read about him from time to time, I don't remember where. I remember thinking, *is he really a rebel or really a do-gooder*?" Sue noted. "What else did he have to say?"

"He advised that if we smoked the one special weed

together that he left me, it would heighten our orgasms."

"Oh yeah!" Sue cried out. "If I screamed any louder the police would arrest you for trying to kill me!"

"Ira believes Abbie is going to make a huge difference. He describes Abbie as a rebel with a conscience for good. Evidently Abbie has already gone down south. He and his people are working on voting rights for Negroes. Sounds very dangerous to me. I hope he doesn't get killed. I wish you had met him.

"After Abbie and Ira left, I checked out Lloyd's. I met two guys who consider themselves regulars. They clued me in about Lloyd's and a few other bars. They basically think that bars are like people. They have personalities and their patrons seem to flock to the bars that fit their personality."

"What are their names? What do they do besides hang out in Lloyd's?"

"Skip and Dick. I didn't ask about their day jobs. I'm not good at describing people, but I'll do my best. Skip was about my height, a trifle heavier. He's somewhat serious looking. Maybe it's the glasses he was wearing. For what it's worth, he has a nice head of dark hair with a touch of gray. I also thought Skip was extremely well spoken. What can one say about bars? But Skip and Dick were able to make some sense of the local ones, just how each one distinguishes itself and draws customers accordingly."

"A touch of gray can be sexy, particularly on a young guy. Anyway, let's get to Dick. How would you best describe him, Mr. Poor Describer?"

"Dick looks close to six feet, or maybe he is. He's handsome in a funny-looking way, sort of Clark Gableish. He has floppy ears, but they seem to fit perfectly. It's his smile that catches you. It radiates and says, 'Let's be friends.'"

"What bothers me is they call themselves 'regulars.' I don't like that. As I've said before, there have to be better places to hang out than bars."

I did not like seeing Sue's eyes narrow, causing deep creases to form in her beautiful forehead.

"Okay, Miss Preachy, let's make up for lost time and forget Lloyd's for the night."

"Love it! I agree about the lost time . . . and especially about a lot of making up to do."

13

NATASHA THE WAITRESS

THE NEXT DAY I brought Gussie two sandwiches. It was early in the day, but Gussie took a substantial bite out of one of them.

"Delish!!" she spat out. "You earned the menus. I did sixty-five for you. More than I promised I'd do. So now take them and beat it."

I wanted to get to Lloyd's early. I had picked up the lettuce and tomatoes. Hopefully the potato salad and coleslaw would be there. Charlie greeted me.

"Hello, 'Fairly Famous.' The salads were just delivered. The butcher brought a mean-looking cooked roast beef over about a half hour ago. I placed it in the oven but didn't turn it on. You'd best check it out. What are you drinking before you get involved with all that? The waitress tonight will be Natasha. I guarantee you'll like her. Hope you brought menus for her."

"Yes, I've got quite a few menus and more in my apartment. I'll take you up on that drink. I'll have a vodka with a squirt of soda and cranberry juice."

Charlie smiled. "What the fuck do you call that concoction?"

I grinned back. "No name."

Charlie handed me the drink as I went off to the kitchen. "Okay, we'll call it the 'Fairly Famous.' Is that okay with you?"

Oh shit! How am I going to handle this? I had never before had to take multiple orders from living customers!!

I looked around. Not much happening yet. Even the jukebox wasn't playing. I hoped it was still early on. Maybe I should wish for a slow evening. This would be my first night taking orders from a real, in the flesh, waitress. I started to slice the roast beef.

"That's for my customers. I want to serve every bit of the roast beef you brought tonight."

I turned and there in front of me was a voluptuous, attractive young woman.

"I'm Natasha. I've been waitressing here the past month. I'm not happy with the little bit of money I've been taking home. If I'm not happy, believe me you won't be happy either. I've had to serve chips with the drinks. I want to serve a lot of sandwiches and salads. Do you get me?"

"We are in total agreement. Let's go to work."

Thirty-eight sandwiches, twenty-five salads, ten potato salads, and five coleslaws later, Natasha came back into the kitchen smiling. She seemed to be warming up to me.

"Not bad for a first night, but we can do better. By the way, a couple just came in from New Jersey. They introduced themselves as Fred and Susan Joseph and as friends of yours from Boston. They ordered three sandwiches. One to take home for their dog. They claim he knows good food when he sniffs it. That takes us to forty-one sandwiches tonight."

Then she glared at me and lowered her voice. "By the way, I'm a Russian maidel. Even Charlie doesn't mess with me."

I lifted up both my hands, signaling surrender. "Okay . . . okay, you take two of the sandwiches out to Fred and Susan. I'll carry out the one for the dog."

I started to head for Fred's table when Sue walked right in front of me with her incredible smile.

"I'm sure you knew I was hungry, and you are bringing me that delicious-looking sandwich."

"Hey, great to see you. No, I didn't know you'd be here tonight, but I'd love you to meet some good friends of mine from Boston. I've known them forever."

As we stood in front of the Joseph table, I welcomed them.

"Hello, Fred and Susan. Please say hello to my good friend Sue."

Susan and Sue smiled at each other.

Sue commented, "I like Susan already, especially her name."

Fred looked past me at Sue. "What's a beautiful girl like you doing with a sandwich maker?"

Sue laughed. "Robert told me you were old friends. That's no way for a friend to talk."

Susan took a bite of her sandwich. "Yum, but the Russian dressing needs a touch of relish. And Sue, if you want to hang out with these two jerks, get ready for the insults. They are both from Dorchester, Mass. where nobody ever talks nice to anybody. Believe me, I know."

"Hey, you two, I'm giving this third sandwich to Sue. If you are serious about one for the dog, I'll slice up another sandwich."

Fred jumped in, "We are. We are serious. This dog knows food. We usually use him as a taster."

"When did you get this dog?" I asked.

"About a month ago. We named him Friskie after the dog I had when I was a kid. Do you remember him? You guys were always pissed at me 'cause I had to walk him. That was usually when you needed me to play stickball or whatever game you were playing at the time. Anyway, Susan and I thought we'd drop by to see how this was going. Looks like it could work, if you don't fuck it up."

Fred turned to Sue and grinned. "Great to meet you. You'd best take good care of our friend here."

Susan smiled at Sue. "Believe me, these Dorchester boys need a lot of help. Just trying to humanize them is a fulltime job."

I ran into the kitchen and very quickly put a sandwich together for Friskie and handed it to Fred.

"I'll be out to visit soon. I can't wait to hear what Friskie thought of the sandwich."

As I headed back to the table to join Sue, Charlie beckoned me to the bar.

"Who were those people? And who is the redhead? You two seemed a little bit more than friendly."

Charlie was tapping his fingers on the bar counter. "Fred is an investment banker. He works for E.F. Hutton."

Charlie sneered, "I thought so. He looks like a banker. We don't get many of his kind in here. Bankers make me nervous."

Charlie went on, "The redhead looks like a nice girl. I don't particularly like 'nice girls.' They make me more nervous than bankers."

I stood there feeling very uncomfortable with what Charlie had just declared.

"Charlie, I am here to make sandwiches. You asked me to be a cook here. I am not trying to please you with my friends who pay for what they eat and drink. That's enough said. Besides, Sue doesn't like bars. You won't be seeing much of her."

Charlie came back at me, "I hope not. I want you to mingle when you aren't making stuff. You know we have a lot of girls coming in here, I can't take care of them all. Just before you arrived, a couple of ladies came in. They introduced themselves as Lois and Sandy. They claimed they knew you and they would be back. Oh, by the way, when you were sitting with your friends, I put a bottle of vodka in the kitchen near your slicer. Guard it with your life."

"I'll do my best. I've never guarded a bottle of vodka before, but I'm pretty sure I can handle it. Maybe I need a rifle?"

"Remember I mentioned Gloria who owns the place? When she comes here, prepare a salad for her with a 'no calorie' dressing. She needs to lose a few pounds, if you get my meaning. By the way, are you balling Sue? Like I pointed out, there is a lot of good stuff coming in here nightly. I'd hate to have to start calling you 'Fairy Famous.'"

Charlie smiled his now somewhat menacing, gap-toothed-smile.

"I hear you. I have to say I never heard the term 'balling' back in Boston. Now I know what Little Richard was really saying when he sang *Good golly, Miss Molly, you sure like to ball.* Good thing the radio networks didn't know either. Anyway, I'll get Sue and we'll walk home. See you tomorrow."

I asked Sue if she was ready to leave.

Sue whispered as she sprang from her seat, "I can't wait to get out of here. I knew I'd hate this place. I just didn't know that I'd hate it this much. Charlie gives me the creeps. Just the way he looked at me. Yuck! If they had played *People* by Barbra Streisand one more time, I think I would have stood up and screamed, 'I hate *People*!!'. She has a screechy voice. I'll bet once Funny Girl is over, she won't be heard from again. Anyway, I'm not coming back soon."

I held the door for her as we left Lloyd's behind. "Sorry, I thought you might like my friends."

"I did like them. Susan was funny, and Fred was a little sarcastic like you. He's quite good looking."

Sue smiled thoughtfully. "Did Charlie say anything about me?"

"No," I lied. "Charlie was mostly speaking about a bottle of vodka he put in the kitchen. Fred would definitely agree about the handsome part. Not sure that he's aware that he's sarcastic. He probably just thinks he's funny."

"The smoke in there was worse than the smoke in the back section of the planes. I thought I might choke to death. Anyway, I did like meeting your friends, so I'll come back if any more come and I'm in town."

"Great. I don't know why, but I have a feeling you

wanted to tell me something privately. I think I'm getting really good at reading your body language."

"Well, the bad news is I got served a summons for disturbing the peace. You probably would have too, but you weren't home when the server came by. It's from our crazy screaming neighbor. Can you believe that she filed a complaint about us? What did we do?"

As Sue shook her head in disbelief, I rolled my eyes.

"The only thing I can possibly think is the noise of my feet on the stairs when I am rushing up to see you."

Sue looked worried. "I guess we'll find out when we show up in court in a few weeks at 9:30 a.m. I'm not sure how to explain this to my supervisor."

I offered, "We can always say jury duty, but if anyone checked, they could probably find out that wasn't true. You might get caught in a lie. How about a bad cold that you don't want to inflict on the passengers?"

Now Sue assured me in return, "We'll think of something before that date."

14

DICK AND SKIP TELL ME

ABOUT BRANDY'S

THE NEXT EVENING, I saw both Skip and Dick. They seemed to be stuck at the bar. They were in the same seats that they were glued to when I met them last Sunday.

"A few days before we met you, both Skip and I got to talking to a couple of girls who are longtime friends. They were at a bar that just opened a few blocks from here. It's called Brandy's. They have a singer named Bobby Hebb there. Pretty spiffy place. Both girls are meeting us here tonight. We'll be ordering a few sandwiches for them and ourselves. They should be here soon. We'll let you know what we think of them."

I grinned. "What you think of the girls?"

"No, the sandwiches, smart ass."

Dick grinned back.

"What did you guys think of Brandy's? What bar personality would you give it?"

Skip jumped in, "Congenial. It was a little like Lloyd's in that it will attract meet-ups, but maybe better. The bartenders were all attractive women. The owners are two guys. One is Jewish named Arnie, the other is Irish, but I didn't get his name. Arnie was very friendly which will help draw customers."

Skip looked over at Dick who was nodding in agreement.

I was very interested in what they were saying.

"Maybe I'll pop over there very soon."

I caught Dick's eye and he gave me a thumbs up. "We already told him about you. He promised to come over and check out your sandwiches. Guess what? They don't have a cook. We heard a couple of Bobby Hebb's songs. Believe me, Mr. Hebb won't hurt their business either."

"Hey, thanks a lot, I really appreciate you promoting me. Did Arnie say when he'd come?"

Skip replied, "No, but he seemed to be listening closely. As Dick mentioned, they don't have a cook, at least not yet."

I looked over at both of them. "By the way, what

are the girls' names?"

Dick was enthusiastic. "My girl is Beverly, she really seemed to like me!"

Skip smiled. "Mine is Yanna. She is a yoga lover. Pardon the pun, but you can bet that's a stretch for me. She talks a yoga streak. I like her okay, but I met another girl at a conference. I was really impressed by her. I'll be bringing her around. Her name is Daryl."

I headed back to the kitchen. Natasha met me before I got there.

"We've sold thirty-two sandwiches so far tonight and only twelve salads. Not sure how many coleslaws or potato salads we've sold. I'm going to the tables that haven't ordered food yet. I'll see what I can round up. Get ready! You may have some serious slicing to do."

I watched Natasha walk over to a couple of tables. She was writing things down on her pad and came back smiling.

"I've got good news. I had forgotten that I had already delivered sandwiches to one of the tables, but the good news is they wanted four more to take home. They were delighted I had come back to their table. Their intent is to bring the sandwiches to their office and share with some of their colleagues. The other table had heard the sandwiches and salads were very good. They ordered two potato salads and two roast beefs."

I smiled. "You are correct. That is very good news."
"Also, I'm not sure if you noticed, but a very nicely

dressed guy just sat down at The Table, the one that the Josephs were at last night. I've got a feeling from the way he's looking around the place that he wants to talk to you or Charlie. You know what, as much as I hate to, I'll put a reserved sign on that table for your friends. But remember, it's your job to see that table eats. You did okay last night with that table. Let's see how you do tonight. Don't forget to ask for tips that are coming to me."

"I'll see if it's me he wants to speak to."

I walked over to The Table where the Josephs had sat. A rather tall, well-groomed guy about thirty stood up slowly and greeted me warmly.

"I'm Arnie Stein. I'm guessing your friends told you about Brandy's. I heard about your food from them and how good it is. I came over to try it and meet you. I'll order a sandwich right now for myself and seven more for my partner, the bartenders, and a few others. If everybody is in agreement that they're good, we'll have something to talk about. The waitress can bring them to me. I know she'll be looking for the tip. One other thing. My partner and I plan to open many bar/restaurants. You could be part of all of this. I'm going to tell you something between you and me . . . between you and me, RIGHT?"

"Yes, of course, just between us."

"Charlie has a very bad rep. He is supposed to be a very jealous guy. It's a can't win situation for you. While he wants you and your food to be popular, he doesn't want you to be more popular than he is. He's thrown out a lot of cooks. Don't forget it, Robert. You may have a novel idea, but you are just a cook in his eyes."

"I appreciate you confiding in me, but I believe I can handle this situation. I've got a nose for trouble. I've seen it all my life. Anyway, I love your plans. I'll get the sandwiches together in a jiffy. How about some salads as well?"

"Nope. Let's get started with the sandwiches and later on we can talk salads."

As I headed back to the kitchen, I saw two attractive women with Skip and Dick.

Dick was pointing at me. The girls were smiling. I walked over to the table where they were sitting.

"I'm Robert. What did these two guys say about me?"

The girl with the gorgeous long legs, bright eyes, and beautiful smile spoke up. "They didn't mention you, but they gave your sandwiches 'very good.' By the way, my name is Beverly. I'd like one of your sandwiches with lettuce and tomato. Could you also put a sliver of cheese in there?"

"I don't have any cheese. Why screw up a delicious sandwich with cheese?"

"You wait," Beverly asserted. "You wait and see. Soon you won't be able to get a sandwich without cheese."

The jukebox was blaring out *Sugar Shack*. Beverly got up and started twisting.

"I love that song," she chirped.

Yanna was laughing and clapping her hands in time to the music.

Yanna declared, "I'm a vegetarian. I'm also a fanatic when it comes to yoga. Robert, do you know anything about yoga?"

"No! Why would I?"

"Why? Why?? You might laugh, but yoga is going to be huge. We live in a very crazy world, full of terrible things happening daily. This is where yoga comes in. Yoga is beneficial for both physical and mental fitness. It's a balancer. And we all need balance. One day it will be endless as to how much good it will be doing. It could even help you now, if you gave it a chance. So, snicker if you will, but take note of my words, Mr. Sandwich Maker. I'll have a lettuce and tomato sandwich, no cheese. Thank you, very much, kind sir."

I waved goodbye to all four of them and headed back to the kitchen.

Poor Skip. I can't imagine listening to all that yoga talk. It would be horrible to marry a yoga fanatic like that. I haven't met Daryl yet, but I already like her better than Yanna.

15

MY BROTHER LOU

MAKES HIS ENTRANCE

THE NEXT EVENING, I left work early. My goal was to figure out how to best set up Brandy's. I had already ordered everything they would need. They didn't have a stove. I would have to cook their roast beef at Lloyd's. One of the bonuses of Lloyd's, was they had a spacious kitchen and a stove that behaved very nicely.

I had been ordering all the beef precooked for Lloyd's as well, but my plan was to quit my day job soon and use Lloyd's stove to cook the beef. This would save quite a bit of money, as Mario, the butcher, charged a lot for cooking the roasts.

As soon as I entered, Arnie jumped up from where he was sitting.

"Hey, Robert, great to see you. Everything you ordered was delivered. My waitresses will cut and serve the sandwiches. They will keep count for me. I'll pay you weekly, whatever the total amount the food brings in. How does that sound?"

I concurred, "Sounds good. It's important to use the 'Fairly Famous' brand for both our sakes."

"Agreed! I'll put 'Fairly Famous' on the menu and even on the napkins. That's what I like about your service. I'm hoping to make you 'VERY Famous.' Only kidding."

Arnie winked.

I hurried back to Lloyd's. I was feeling pretty good about the deal I just made with Arnie. I waved at Charlie as I walked toward the kitchen. Natasha was already blocking the kitchen entrance.

She blurted out impatiently, "I hope we'll sell more sandwiches than last night. We only did forty-six last evening and thirty salads including the potato salad and coleslaw."

I thought that was a good number. I doubted there would ever be enough sandwiches sold for Natasha. However, before I could respond and ask about her tips, I heard someone bellowing at Charlie.

"How about a Johnny Walker Black on the rocks and a drink for your cook, if you know what the hell he's drinking."

I took a look over at the bar. It was my brother Lou.

He saw me gawking at him.

"I came here to test your sandwiches and to buy you a drink," he growled.

Charlie piped up, "He's drinking vodka with cranberry juice and a touch of soda. We call the drink 'Fairly Famous.' We named it after Robert. We don't have Johnny Black. Will Red do?"

"Sure, I like them both. But how my kid brother came up with that bullshit drink, I'll never know. I'll take a sip after you make it and bring it over to him."

The next thing Lou was standing in front of me holding my drink.

"I'm going to buy six sandwiches to take home. I hope for your sake that they're good. Here's your drink. I tried it. I almost spat it out. There's a scotch waiting for me at the bar. I'm going to get it. I'll talk to the bartender, if you don't mind?"

"I'll be making up your sandwiches. Natasha will carry them over to you. Don't forget to tip her."

"You are telling me not to forget to tip her?? You can kiss my you know what! I was tipping before you were born!"

While I was making up the sandwiches, I could hear Lou bellowing to Charlie.

"I thought I taught him better. Once in a while on Saturdays, I'd meet him in downtown Boston. While I was working with my friend Nick, the pattern maker, he'd get a haircut with Joe, the barber that I used. When I finished, we'd go over to the hotel bar across from South Station. I'd order two scotches, one for him and one for me. The bartenders would look at Bobby and say, 'Your friend looks a little young.' Bobby was probably sixteen or seventeen at the time. By the way, we all called Robert, Bobby, in Boston. My answer was always the same, 'He's not my friend, he's my older brother. He just looks young.' Then I'd turn to Bobby and ask, 'What did you tell Joe today?' Bobby always made up the same thing, 'I told him you were not a real brother. My parents were digging up clam shells on some beach and found you and took you home.' I loved that story. It always gave me a big laugh. Then I'd tell him, 'I'll straighten that barber out. I'll tell him the truth. You were the one found on the beach. It was you our parents took home.'"

Charlie smiled. "Both you guys are pretty good fabricators, but that still doesn't tell me how Robert came up with that concoction for a drink."

I watched as Lou left, yelling, "I'll let you know the verdict on your sandwiches."

Later that evening Natasha let me know that we hit fifty-one sandwiches, and twenty-eight salads.

"Your brother helped the count. He's very nice looking. I love his deep voice."

That evening the phone rang. It was Lou.

"You passed the test out here in Hillsdale. Everybody loved your sandwiches. Only one complaint. I should have brought more home. I think you might have something going there. Stick with it. That's my only advice. Remember bars are seductive in many ways, so keep your nose clean. Try not to fuck around too much."

16

MY DAD CHECKS IN

I WENT TO sleep on that "not fucking around" note. The next day would be Saturday. I would need my sleep, especially if I were going to "fuck around." As I was getting set to leave for Lloyd's, the phone rang.

"It's me, your father. Do you remember me? We haven't spoken in a very long while. What's going on? Your brother Lou called me last night. He told me he picked up a bunch of sandwiches from you in a BAR? He added that you had moved the business from your apartment. Now everybody in the family knows. They're all sick with worry. Your sister Charlotte is very, very upset. She will call you later."

"Dad, I'm not a child. I know what I'm doing. Since when does my family know what's good for me? You know I don't like my day job. I'm hoping to make this idea work. If it does, bar or no bar, everybody will be pleased with their brother Bobby."

"Ever since you went traipsing off to New York, you have given me nothing but worry. Is that girl still with you? What was her name? That tramp! Do you remember your sister Jean wouldn't invite you or her to our summer party? We heard that she was living with you. I remember how nauseous we all felt when we found out her shoes were under your bed."

"The tramp's name was and is 'Pat.' She's back at school. We broke up a while ago. It wasn't a pleasant break-up, but she's not a tramp, Dad. Give me some credit. She was anything but a tramp. Besides, Dad, you wanted me to move to New York City. You advised that it would be good for me. I said that I didn't want to go. I didn't want to go for that stupid job!"

"Only you could find a non-Jewish girl in New York City, with the name 'Pat,' yet! New York City has more Jewish girls than Israel. Anyway, I'm surprised you ever listened to me. It was always your mother who let you get away with everything. Your mother ruined you through and through. Even though she's been gone for a few years, it's her voice you listen to, not mine. C'mon home. You'll find a job here you'll like. For once listen to your father."

"Dad, I'm not coming home. I'm not ever coming back to your home. This is my home. I like it here. I may be successful here, or may not. This is where I live. This is where I will stay."

"I knew I'd be wasting my breath on you. Do what you want. You always have!"

My father grunted as we both hung up.

I was surprised he had called on a Saturday. That was his day to have some friends over for lox, bagels, cream cheese and, of course, one card game or another. I could still sniff the wonderful aroma of the half sour pickles. I didn't miss much of Dorchester, but I did miss those Saturdays, when I didn't go into Boston. One of the best parts about those Saturdays was the 'kibitzers.' They had something sarcastic to say about everything and usually everybody.

I closed the door behind me and headed off to Lloyd's.

It's not easy to please everyone, besides that's not my job. I had explained to my father what I was doing and why. It's not my responsibility how he deals with it!

It was the best day at Lloyd's. I lost the exact count, but I knew it was over sixty sandwiches.

Natasha looked me over. "You look exhausted. I'll finish up the night for you and give you the exact count later. You know you can trust me."

I called Arnie at Brandy's. He picked up the phone right away.

"Brandy's had a good night for Fairly Famous. We

sold thirty-six sandwiches."

"Thanks, I'll come by early tomorrow and check to see if everything is set up and ready for another good night!"

I headed back to my place. Sue had the weekend off.

I called her.

"How is tomorrow to get together?" I asked.

"It should be fine, but I was hoping to see you tonight. Are you feeling okay?"

"I'm okay, just very, very tired. I'm thinking, I could be at your place about 2:00 p.m."

"That will work. You can tell me tomorrow why you are so tired. I hope it's not what I'm thinking."

"I don't have any idea what your fuzzy brain is thinking, but I'll be up there at 2:00. I'll be doing some serious defuzzing."

Sue whispered, "I can't wait. I always wanted to get defuzzed."

17

ESTHER NAN MAKES

HER FIRST APPEARANCE

THE NEXT DAY, I made it over to Brandy's at 11:00 a.m. Arnie was waiting for me.

He spoke right up. "Great to see you. Let's check out the kitchen and see if we need anything today."

"Sounds good to me."

We walked into the kitchen. There were two roasts there. I counted eighty rolls and plenty of condiments.

Arnie smiled. "I believe we are in good shape for today and tomorrow. You keep missing my partner. Pretty soon you will think he doesn't exist."

As I waved goodbye I said, "Not a problem. I'm sure I'll meet him soon enough. See you soon."

I thought I'd stop by Lloyd's to say hello to Jake. It was still early, not quite 12:00 p.m. It would be a nice walk as well. I'd be at Sue's by 2:00 p.m. Not a problem. Jake was in the kitchen. He was looking very pleased, but as he spotted me, he looked puzzled.

"What are you doing here on a Sunday?"

"Thought I'd come by and say hello to you. Any sales yet?" I pointed at the slicer.

Jake smiled happily. "Yup, it started early. See that young girl sitting at the bar? Her name is Esther Nan Bell. She got here about a half-hour ago. Esther Nan mentioned that she was very hungry. She had missed her breakfast catching a train from Poughkeepsie early this morning. Esther Nan hates train food. She tries to come into the city most weekends. She says, 'Whether I'm hungry or not.'"

Jake continued, "Anyway, the guy next to her is her 'boyfriend.' His name is Tedd, with two Ds. Get that 'two Ds'. He claims that's because of Actor's Equity. They already had a Ted with his last name and only one D. He's a roommate of that phony, pompous Billy. They both study acting at The Neighborhood Playhouse. Last week Tedd had to go out for about fifteen minutes to call his 'agent.' He must have called from the phone booth across the street. At least it gave me a chance to talk to Esther Nan. First of all, she is very nice, even though she goes to Vassar. She is from Marblehead Mass. of all places to be from. Did you ever see bigger brown eyes? Maybe Audrey Hepburn?"

"She's cute alright. I'll bet anything that Tedd is an asshole, since he rooms with Billy. He also looks way too old for little missy Bell. More importantly, I hope she liked the sandwich?"

"She must have. She gobbled up one last week along with your 'Fairly Famous' salad. She didn't order a salad today, but she did order two sandwiches a few minutes ago. She asked me to wrap up one of them for her to take back to school. She added, 'No onions, please. I'll be eating it on a train.' She's even very considerate."

"She probably didn't order a salad today because you made the salad and not me." I laughed. "Anyway, I hope she's not sleeping with that jerk."

Jake protested, "Hey, you don't even know him!"

I snorted. "I don't have to know him. Just being Billy's roommate speaks volumes."

"Oh yeah!" Jake countered. "You were my roommate for a few weeks and I'm still a very nice guy despite knowing you.

"Marblehead, hmmm. My brother David has a sailboat moored up there. I wonder if she's a sailor? Vassar, huh? I don't know anybody up there. Oh well, poor girl will never get to know me."

I frowned. Jake smirked.

"All I can say is that she doesn't know how lucky she is." Jake continued to smirk.

"Anyway, I promised Sue I'd meet her at 2:00 p.m. Oh, before I go, did you notice a bottle of vodka near the slicer? Charlie put it there. He seriously instructed us to guard it with our lives."

"Yuh, I noticed it last week. I didn't see it this week. You should know yourself. You tend to clutter. Why do you think he put one bottle of vodka there? He has a ton of vodka bottles at the bar."

Jake shrugged as he pointed to the clutter.

"Lord only knows. I'll tell you what I've heard about Charlie sometime this week. I'll give you a call."

18

SUE GETS TO KNOW

ABOUT MY FAMILY

I WALKED BACK to my apartment. I'd be a little early for Sue. I didn't think she'd mind.

As soon as I got to my room, I called her.

"Hey there, can I come up now?"

"Hey there, yourself," Sue retorted. "Get yourself up here. I want to see if I've been missing anything."

Sue's laugh was warm and inviting.

The door was open and Sue was in the kitchen.

"I prepared us some Midwestern food. Egg salad with lots of mayo and celery. I also have toasted white bread. I've gotten to learn how you Jewish guys feel about white bread. Regarding the mayonnaise, you've already told me how you feel about mayonnaise. So I bought Hellman's. I saw a woman next to me buy Cain's mayo. I figured she wasn't Jewish, or her boyfriend wasn't Jewish. Anyway, let's talk. We haven't seen each other for at least a week. What's going on with you, my dear?"

"Well, I hooked up with another bar. Basically, I'll be catering for them, but I'll still be at Lloyd's. On the other news front, one of my older brothers visited me at Lloyd's. Mmm! Yummy egg salad. I'll take a few more scoops. Must be the mayo."

"What older brother? What do you mean one of your older brothers? You never mentioned that you had any siblings!"

Sue sounded exasperated.

"Sorry, you are right. I haven't talked much about them."

"Much!" Sue cried. "You haven't shared a word about your family."

"Well, I guess I've been so busy talking and thinking about 'Fairly Famous' and your beautiful body that I just didn't get to my family yet."

"In that order? 'Fairly Famous' and then my body? That will get you nowhere, my friend."

Sue's eyes twinkled as she took a hard bite of her sandwich.

"Okay, okay, I'm the youngest of seven. There were five boys and two girls. I also have fifteen nephews and nieces."

"What do you mean there were five boys and two girls?"

"I came very late. My oldest sister Jean was a sophomore in college when I appeared. My brother Hank was two years younger than Jean. He enlisted in the Army Air Corps when he was twenty-one. He flew in a B-26. It got shot down with only a few weeks left in the European war. We never heard from him again. We had a letter from him the day before his plane was struck. He wrote how lucky he was to have such a terrific crew. He told us, 'These guys are the best. We keep each other safe from harm's way.' That letter and a picture of him and his crew got hung up in our hallway and is most likely there now."

I brushed the sandwich crumbs from my pants, took a deep breath and continued.

"I could only remember meeting him once or twice. Once when Hank was home on furlough, I was sitting on the toilet looking up at him as he shaved.

'How is Kindergarten?' Hank asked.

'Horrible.'

'Why?'

Hank looked down at me with a puzzled expression. I whimpered, 'Because they make me sing a song that I hate.'

Hank looked back down at me, 'Tell them you aren't going to sing it anymore!'

"The next day I told the teacher that I hated the song and that I didn't want to sing it ever again. The teacher promptly sent me home with a note to my mother detailing how poorly I had behaved.

"My brother Paul also enlisted. He was a navigator. His squadron flew B17s. He told us that we should not try to find out about Hank. The rumors had been gruesome. If the civilians captured you after you bailed out of a plane, it was probably a very ugly story. The civilians were furious at our bombing raids. At that time, the Gestapo knew the war was almost over. If a parachuted flyer got caught by the Gestapo, they would be brought back safely to a prisoner of war camp. I guess Hank wasn't so lucky."

I grimaced as I shook my fist fruitlessly in the air.

"Paul was about two years younger than Hank. They were the best of friends."

Sue reached over and gently touched my cheek.

"I can't begin to tell you how sorry I am. I'm so sorry that you didn't get to know him better."

"Lou is about three years younger than Paul. He also enlisted in the Army Air Corps. He was a mechanic. His job was to check planes before they went overseas. He was the last member of my family to see Hank before he left for Europe. He tried very hard to arrange a meeting in Bangor, Maine for all of us to say goodbye to

Hank. The meeting had to be a complete secret. Nobody was supposed to know who was going where, especially flight crews. Anyway, Hank's plane took off before we got there. Our car broke down half-way up to Bangor.

"My mother never forgave my dad for us having left late in the morning. She also was very upset that my father didn't have the car checked a few days before.

"Lou was disappointed that the air force would not allow three brothers to be overseas at the same time. He frequently pushed for his commanding officer to make an exception, but he was always knocked back. The commanding officer would apparently scratch his head and wonder out loud, 'You Jews are supposed to be smart. Why the hell would you want to go over there and get yourself killed?'"

Sue interrupted, "Your brothers were all very brave. My dad would be shocked. He always maintained that Jews never served in the war."

Sue shrugged her shoulders.

Then she said tenderly, as she intertwined her hands with mine, "What a terrible loss Hank must have been for all of you. I'm so very sorry you didn't get to see him off."

"In my case, your dad is right. I don't like what we are doing in Vietnam. There are going to be a lot of lives lost there for no good reason that I can understand. I didn't want mine to be one of them . . . Jew or no Jew!"

My voice was breaking. I rose and took the plate

that had been holding my sandwich over to the sink.

"Delicious, even though it was a Midwest sandwich."

I threw Sue a kiss.

"There are still more war stories. My dad was actually in the Air Force at the very beginning of the first World War."

"I had no idea we actually had an air force in WWI."

Sue was surprised.

I agreed, "I know what you mean. Can you imagine what those planes looked like back then?"

We both laughed.

"He loved to reassure my mother, 'Do you know how far those new war planes have come, compared to the ones I flew in during the First Big War? That's why we don't have to worry. Our boys will be safe. Those planes will keep them safe.'

"My mother's contribution was to hang three stars in the front window to show people how proud she was of her three sons that were serving the nation and, perhaps, the world. It's hard to imagine how frightened she must have been.

"I had it easy in the Army Reserve I was actually stationed near where my father had served at Kelly Air Force Base. I was at an Army base called Fort Sam. In San Antonio.

"My mother passed away while I was there. I was granted emergency leave to go home. My brother Lou was friendly with the man who dropped the second bomb on Japan. His name was Charles Sweeney. He was still in the Reserves. He was then a Major General. Somehow my brother Lou got him to pilot a plane to pick me up and take me to Boston for my mother's funeral. It was the worst ride I ever experienced. I was so choked up. I barely spoke."

Sue placed her hand on my fingers and squeezed them lightly. "I'm so sorry for how you must have felt. I wish I could have been there for you."

"Can you imagine just me alone with a real live General? He was also very famous or to some people—infamous. As I said before, he flew the B-29 that dropped the nuclear bomb on Nagasaki. The bomb was called "The Fat Man" because of its round shape. I had no idea how to try and start a conversation."

Sue tapped her forehead. "You did the absolute right thing. You shut the hell up! I hope you were able to take a little nap."

I yawned and nodded. "My brother David, who is about five years older than me, served in Korea in the so- called 'Korean Police Action.' They didn't have window stars during the 'Korean Police Action' or she would have hung one for David."

Sue exclaimed, "I can't believe that we've been sleeping together since almost the first day we met. That was months ago and I'm just finding all this out now. No! I cannot even try to imagine how worried your mom had to be. Every day! Every night! What about you? You were a very little boy. What was it like for you?"

Sue moved her whole body closer to mine.

"Well, I don't know that much about you either. In fact, zero, except maybe the little you've told me about your parents and their thoughts about Jews."

"In my case, there isn't that much to tell, but you have this humongous family. Did you get along with each other?" Sue asked with a very puzzled expression.

"Well, sometimes," I quipped. "Paul was our oldest brother after Hank was killed. He had flown over fifty missions and won the Distinguished Flying Cross. After he was discharged, he graduated from M.I.T. He married Ruth Shultz and they went on to have four children. He was a hero to all of us. We were good friends even though he was considerably older than me. I spent a lot of time at Paul and Ruth's home in Newton, Mass.

"I used to pick up hot fudge sundaes for them. While they were smacking their lips on the ice cream drowned in hot fudge and marshmallow, I'd ask if the sundaes were better than sex. They would just smile and continue to smack their lips in delight." I imitated the smacking sound. "David was closest to me in age. We got to like each other better after he married my sister-in-law, Lorraine. I remember once bringing them more steamers than the three of us could eat. We all laughed that the steamers won the battle.

"I have two sisters. Charlotte is eight years older

than me. We got to be good buddies washing the dinner dishes together. We shared a lot of secrets."

"Secrets? You are a very secretive fellow. I've let you put your whanger inside me, but it is very hard to get inside of you."

"Believe me. I am more than thankful about you permitting me entrance.

"There is more about Charlotte. I used to love to drive to her house. We would talk and talk about books, movies, and our nutty family. Charlotte had read a lot more than I had. She loved to teach me what she knew. She wanted so much to become a teacher. Usually before I left for the evening, I would open their refrigerator door and mostly just stare inside. It made her husband Harold crazily pissed. He was not happy with my visits.

"I'm trying my very best to reveal some of my past. I haven't mentioned Jean yet. I probably didn't get there because I figured you'd be bored."

I looked away.

"BORED?" Sue hollered, her mouth opened wide. "I'm loving it! Tell me more."

"Jean is the oldest child. She was a sophomore at the University of New Hampshire when I was born. She has always been very serious. Her life has never been easy. A lot of it is her own making. However, in spite of many obstacles, Jean became a teacher. She is much sought after in a good way by many students.

"Her husband Ben is a great guy. He's a social worker and from my perspective is a very patient man. As an outsider coming into my family, that's a very important quality to have. Ben also owned a racing bike which I coveted. For whatever his reason, Ben granted me the bicycle 'for keeps.' He evidently also had great foresight since I'd ride the bike to pick up a rye bread for my house and deliver one to Ben and Jean almost every day.

"And Lou, he is married to Jackie. Jackie was born in Ireland. She has a way of pronouncing words with a touch of a brogue. Whenever Jackie listens to someone's tale of woe, she loves to say 'win some, lose some' again with the slightest hint of the brogue. They have four children but none of them speak with a brogue.

"Lou is doing very well as a salesman. None of us are surprised. I don't know about you, but I'm bored with this bio."

I waved my hand at Sue.

"Maybe you are bored because you already know all this."

"Anyway, let's get back to 'Robert's Fairly Famous' and your body. Yes, in that order.

"The new bar calls itself Brandy's. One of the owners is Arnie. He agrees with you about Charlie. He says Charlie has a reputation of being paranoid and jealous. His point is that I can't win. If I don't do a good job, he'll throw me out. If I do too good a job, he'll be very jealous. He'll make false accusations and throw me out. Arnie called it a lose/lose."

I grunted.

Sue murmured, "This is also a no win for me. I disliked Charlie from the moment I laid eyes on him. But another stinking bar! More drunken people! Is this what you want? And very selfishly, less time with me."

Sue placed her hands on her lap.

"Sue, I know. You are right. I will be very busy, but I'll always find time for us."

I got up and kissed Sue's cheek.

"Thanks a lot. I have an idea. Let's go back to our beginnings. You go back to your apartment, close your eyes and wait for my stomps."

Sue slapped the bed. I rocketed down the steps. If we were going to replay our very first sexual encounter, I'd make a few changes. I checked out my underpants and my pants zipper. As much as I loved and cherished my first exciting night with Sue, I didn't want my penis to get stuck in the zipper again. Also, this time I would ask her where to start. Top or bottom?

The stomp came. Actually, it was a double stomp. I flew up the stairs and her door was partially open. She was on the bed totally naked.

As I began to remove my shirt, I whispered, "What if someone else came in? Your door was a tiny bit open."

Sue smirked, "I'd have to fight him or her off. Anyway, I figured you'd be along soon. You could then be my shining knight. Right?"

Sue patted the bed again, motioning me to join her.

"Feet first?" I asked as I pointed at her feet.

"You go wherever you want. I'll be wherever you go and happy to be there."

She waved her arms for me to hurry.

We fell asleep in each other's arms. We both knew something was pending. We both knew it wouldn't be good for either of us. We held each other very tightly.

19

ABBIE HOFFMAN

MAKES AN OFFER

MONDAY ARRIVED BEFORE I was ready for it. I had made up my mind that I would tell my boss that I had to leave. I'd ask if he needed me to stay to train someone. It seemed that all my fellow workers had read my mind. Everybody that I spoke to in the office seemed ready to say goodbye. Mostly they asked if I'd sold a lot of sandwiches over the weekend.

One fellow, who sat in the next office, was one of those perpetual nose pickers. Even worse, he was an examiner of his product. As I poked my head into his office, he took his eyes off his fingers and flapped his hand at me. "I don't have any beef with you, even if you are leaving us."

I wasn't sure if I should duck. I was always worried what might fly off his hands. I heard him cackling as I returned to my cubby hole. He most likely thought saying he didn't have any "beef" with me was very funny.

I sat at my desk wondering if I was doing the right thing. My wondering came to an abrupt end. My boss was suddenly hovering over me. He glared.

"The word is out! I heard you will be quitting today."

I looked up at him. "Yes, I had planned on telling you this morning."

"You've had a lot of the morning to tell me, but you haven't. Now I'm going to tell you! I'm not going to ask you for any notice."

He continued, still glaring at me, "Amanda will be replacing you. You two have done some work together in the past. She feels she can step right into your spot. You may as well pack up your things and shuffle off."

I reached out to shake his hand. He reluctantly shook my hand and pulled away.

I had no idea what more there was to say. I thought I'd take his advice and shuffle off.

I headed to Lloyd's and met Gloria for the very first time. As I walked into the bar, Charlie put his hand over his mouth and pointed in the direction of a rather stout lady seated at a table by herself, smoking a cigarette.

He whispered, "That's Gloria."

She was pretty much what I had envisioned: somewhat overweight with a round face and small features. She looked quite a bit older than me. She was probably at least thirty-five.

Gloria made clear that she would be meeting someone very soon, but asked if I would make her one of those salads people were raving about before she left. She crushed out her cigarette and smiled.

"Please, nothing fancy. I'm on a very strict diet. Very pleased with what I'm hearing about your food. Keep on cooking."

I quickly flew into the kitchen. I cut the tomatoes and shredded the lettuce as carefully as I could. I then proceeded to add my 'Robert's' dressing. Nothing but olive oil, lemon, and dill. I looked down at it as I brought it to her. *What I handed to her was truly a thing of beauty.* I went back to the kitchen where I was still able to watch her gulp it down, seemingly with pleasure, and then she scooted hurriedly out the door.

***

The next couple of nights proceeded well. Business in both places kept increasing. Then it was Thursday night, not too early to start thinking about Sunday. All of a sudden, the jukebox began playing *We Shall Overcome*. I wondered what that song was still doing there. Charlie hated it. I looked over at Charlie. He was grimacing.

"I told that jukebox guy to remove that fuckin' song."

Charlie banged his fist on the bar. Natasha grabbed my hand and pointed to The Table that she reserved for my friends.

"That's Abbie Hoffman!" She was awestruck, but concerned as she whispered, "Charlie is not going to be happy. Abbie states he's a friend of yours. He asked me to find you."

Natasha looked over at Charlie.

"Thanks."

I slipped over to where Abbie was sitting.

"Hey, great to see you!" I exclaimed, as I put my hand on Abbie's shoulder.

"You too!" said a grinning Abbie. "I was hoping to talk to you about some serious issues."

Abbie was altogether more serious than the last time I saw him.

"Okay, what's up?"

I put my hand down and placed it on The Table.

Abbie began, "You seem to be in your own world here. I see a lot of girls. Music. You'll notice I just played *We Shall Overcome*, but there is more to the world than this. I'm hooking up with Students for a Democratic Society in a few weeks. We are going down south to see if we can make some important changes. That's just the beginning. There is a fucking war going on in Vietnam. I don't think President Johnson knows what he's fuckin' with or who he's fuckin' with. There is a lot to be done. Will you come with me? By the way, I guarantee a lot of pussy down there."

Abbie did a thumbs up with both his hands.

"I'd love to, but I'm just starting out with this business. What would I live on?"

"We'll take care of the food and drink and whatever else you'll need. Think about it. I don't need a decision tonight."

Abbie put his hand out and instead of shaking my hand, he grabbed my arm and raised it. It was almost like he had me saluting him.

"Think about it."

Abbie let go of my arm and sauntered out of Lloyd's. Charlie rushed over to me before I could get up. "Was that who I think it was? He's a pinko, liberal troublemaker. Is that fucker a friend of yours?"

Charlie glared and me and then snarled, "I assume he is, or otherwise I would have eighty-sixed him. You know what it means to eighty-six someone, Robert? It means get the fuck out and don't fuckin come back again!!"

Charlie banged his fist on The Table.

"I doubt that he'll be back soon. He's going off in a couple of weeks. Yes, he is a friend of mine and I'm glad he came to visit me."

I sat up in my chair and continued.

"My job is to please people with my food. It's not my job to please you with my friends or my politics."

"Sorry. I lost it, Robert. I just don't like hippies."

Charlie opened his fist and rubbed a crumb off The Table.

I nodded. "I understand. Not everybody agrees on much today. We are in for some turbulent times."

I stood up and headed back to the kitchen.

***

It seemed I was having nightly visitors at Lloyd's. I think a lot of my friends thought this was a colorful life compared to what they were doing. Peter Weiss had called me late last night to tell me he was coming to the city on business. He was working for a shoe manufacturer in Salem, Mass. where his dad was the factory's foreman. Peter had customers in New York, then he would go on to St. Louis. I asked Sue if she'd be around to meet with him. I very much wanted Peter to meet Sue. Perhaps I wanted to show Sue off. I wouldn't mind too much if Pete were jealous. Also, Peter and I had been friends for many years. I thought Sue might enjoy him and what he had to say.

"What time did he say he'd be there? I don't want to spend one minute more at Lloyd's than to just say hello to your friends."

I had told Peter what Fred had asked when he met Sue. I asked Peter not to ask the same question. I also told Peter that Sue was a TWA flight attendant.

Surprisingly, they both arrived at the same time. Peter took one look at Sue and asked, "What's a beautiful girl like you doing with Robert here?"

"Are you from Dorchester too?"

Sue scowled as she turned to me. "Do all your friends go to the college for jerky insults?" Sue threw her hands up in mock desperation.

Peter chimed in, "No, I'm from Swampscott. Hope you'll be on my flight tomorrow. I'm flying TWA to St. Louis. Robert and I are old ski buddies. I'll never forget the time when we were at the top of the mountain on a ski lift. Robert had fallen asleep when it was time to get off. He had to stay on all the way back to the bottom."

Peter was laughing.

Sue smiled at Peter. "I'm going to Chicago, but if I were going to St. Louis, I'd pump you for details about growing up with Robert. Robert tells me very little about himself. I never even knew that he skied. Anyhow, I told Robert I'd only stay a few minutes. I'll leave you two gents to talk about old times."

Sue turned and left and I watched her walk out.

"She's a winner." Peter groaned. "I'm so jealous. Recently, I met this incredible girl in Boston. Her name is Ronnie. We had some amazing times together this past summer. Then she went back to school and we broke up."

Suddenly Peter's face looked very sad. "What school?" I asked.

"University of Michigan," moaned Peter.

"You got to be shitting me."

"Why? Why would I shit you about a break-up that's got me so frigging depressed?"

Peter wiped his hands on a napkin.

"Because, my man, I just went through almost the identical story. This beautiful, really smart girl came in from the University of Michigan and spent the entire summer with me in my apartment not far from here. At summer's end, she went back to school. We carried on a long-distance relationship for a very short time. I was lucky. The amazing Sue came along. She lives right over me in my building. Sue has healed most of my wounds."

I smiled and nodded, then banged The Table. "Maybe there is something about the University of Michigan. Maybe it puts hexes on long-distance relationships. Oh, by the way, Swampscott and Marblehead abut, right? The reason I mention that is last Sunday a very pretty young girl named Esther Nan Bell came in here. I was told she is from Marblehead. Do you know her? Have you heard the name before?"

"Never heard of the girl, but there is a Bell Olds not far from Swampscott. Maybe that's her family? Well, anyway, maybe I'll get lucky too. Rub my forehead. Perhaps the good luck will rub off. I'm off to get some sleep. I'd better be ready for those buyers tomorrow."

"Hey, Pete, before you leave, I've got to tell you how much I liked visiting your house in Swampscott.

Yes, I liked the house, where it was set overlooking the ocean. I liked your parents, especially your mother. Best of all, I loved that you had another refrigerator in your basement. I especially loved that your parents kept it full of cold cuts, marvelous slices of Corned Beef, turkey, salami, and half sour pickled tomatoes. I used to think I could turn your basement into my home. What more would I need?"

I rubbed my stomach, as I added, "Yum, yum! What brought that to mind is I just finished reading *Goodbye Columbus*. The writer, Phillip Roth, is sneaking around his girlfriend Brenda's house and discovers a refrigerator full of fruit. Not bad I thought, but I'll take the cold cuts any day! Good luck tomorrow."

I gave Peter a little push and added, "Have fun."

20

MY SISTER CHARLOTTE AND AN OLD FRIEND

THE WEEK WENT by without much change. Business was doing well in both places. Frank Morse called me on Friday and let me know he'd stop by on Monday. Frank and I had been friends for a long time. We had actually been co-counselors at a co-ed camp.

Saturday morning I was awakened by the ringing phone. I was sure it was my dad again. It wasn't. It was my sister Charlotte.

"Dad called me this morning to say how worried he is that you are working in a bar."

"I know. I heard it all from him last Saturday. There are probably better places to work out of than bars, but right now they are selling quite a few sandwiches. I've had a lot of friends from home drop by. They believe what I'm doing is very exciting."

"Are you in more than one bar?"

"Well, sort of. I'm in one and catering for a second one."

"Anyway, I really didn't call to talk about bars. I'm sure you know what you are doing. If not, you will find out very quickly. I heard that you and Pat broke up. Sorry that I never got to meet her. David and Lorraine did. They liked her a lot. What happened?"

"Long distance relationships. They are very clumsy, especially if you are a pretty girl and surrounded by smart, horny guys. She probably decided she could do better, but then she never had a chance to try one of my roast beef sandwiches."

"I'm not worried about you. I'm sure that if what you are doing doesn't work out the way you want it to, then you'll do something else that will. Before I hang up and I know it's none of my business, but have you replaced Pat yet?"

"Well, sort of. Hard to replace those Hungarian dishes that Pat put together. I still miss the beef stroganoff. The palatschinken she served for dessert were the yummiest. They made up for not having the crepes you used to make for me. But mostly everything else is in place. Her name is Sue. She is spectacularly nice. She's from the Midwest. You know that Midwest people have a reputation for being 'nice.' Sue is the embodiment of nice. She's a stewardess for TWA. I believe brother David would like her too. She's quite pretty."

"I'll bet one day Pat will regret breaking off with you. Speaking of regrets, Harold does not miss your visits to our refrigerator." Charlotte laughed.

"You are 'my dear baby brother.' I know I don't ever have to spend even one minute worrying about you. You know how to take care of Bobby or should I now say 'Robert'? Love you. I'm telling you goodbye with a kiss all the way from Brookline, Mass."

"Sending one right back. Thanks for your confidence in me. I surely need it and appreciate it."

I felt myself smiling.

***

Frank Morse kept his word. He showed up about nine-thirty on Monday evening.

Natasha called out to me, "Check out The Table. Somebody named Frank is awaiting your presence while waiting for two especially thick roast beefs."

As Natasha sauntered off, she stopped at the jukebox. She glanced over at Charlie and played *You Don't Own Me*. I wasn't crazy about Leslie Gore, neither as a singer nor as a songwriter, but I thought the lyrics were appropriate.

"I asked Frank if he wanted any food," Natasha announced. "Frank responded, 'The cook here is my buddy Robert. He knows me and my appetite very well. We were co-counselors at a camp in Maine. Every night one of us would bring back two huge burgers for the other one. It didn't matter what time of night or even morning, or if we had fallen asleep. They were gobbled like we had never seen food before. On that note, I'll have two of Robert's thickest roast beefs and a potato salad and coleslaw. And I'll have your house beer.' Frank pushed his chair forward and smiled at me as he dictated that order."

I sliced his sandwiches and made my way over to The Table.

"Frank, great to see you."

I placed the sandwiches in front of Frank. Natasha brought over the salads.

"Haven't seen you in a long while. What's up?" I asked.

"I'm heading home to Brookline next weekend. My parents have been bugging me to meet this girl, Nina. Her parents are friends of my parents. They belong to the same country club. Our 'Mothers' generally sunbathe poolside. They usually spend about five-minutes discussing the problems of the world. When they realize they can't do anything for the world they decide to fix us by fixing us up. Nina's parents are celebrating an anniversary next weekend. My folks will be there and so will this Nina person. Evidently Nina will be coming in from her school. I believe she goes to Vassar. So, it's not like a fix-up or a date/date. It's just a meet-up."

I snorted. "Sounds pretty 'hoity-toity' to me. Will the celebration be at the country club? Anyway, if you marry Nina, I may have to call it an 'arranged' marriage."

Frank grinned. "I'm not marrying anyone, including the French girl I just spent the weekend with. She has a huge crush on Jean-Paul Belmondo. Are you ready for this? I reminded her of Belmondo. I'll take second best to him any weekend, which by the way was a fabulous weekend."

"I'm not surprised that your parents are fixing you up, so to speak. Your dad and mother were different than any other parents I had met. In some ways, I thought they were cool. I remember they had cocktails and appetizers before they sat down for their dinner. So typically not Jewish. I always thought your father was the first WASP Jew I ever met. He hated me. I could sense he thought I was too Jewish-looking and too Jewish acting to fit his taste, or whoever he wanted you to buddy up with. One evening, as I was leaving your house, I inadvertently half closed the door behind me. He yelled, 'What? Were you brought up in a barn!!' I was all of eighteen. It's one of those hurts that are difficult to brush off."

"Yes, I guess he could be harsh at times. But you and I were and are good friends. I would never let anyone take that away from us, not even my dad."

I reminisced, "Your mum was nice to me. She would always offer me a drink when they were having their sips. Hey, I'd also appreciate it if you would remember to ask this Nina if she knows somebody named Esther Nan Bell up at Vassar. Esther was visiting Lloyd's last Sunday. Everybody noticed her. My partner Jake got to speak with her the weekend before and thought she was quite lovely. Her name alone is intriguing."

Frank asked to borrow my pen. He wrote Esther's name on a napkin and stuffed it in his pocket. He finished all his food and smacked his lips.

"That was delicious, but not quite as good as being awakened at midnight, blinking my eyes open and seeing you offer me two juicy burgers. I never had a problem getting back to sleep either. I'll let you know about the party and Nina when I return."

Frank handed me back the pen.

"Sounds good to me. Travel safe and don't blow your nose in that napkin."

21
GOING TO COURT WITH SUE

WHEN I GOT home, I called Sue.

"I'm thinking about our being in court tomorrow. Let's meet downstairs at eight-thirty, semi-sharp. What did you tell your supervisor?"

"The truth. I told her that I had a crazy lady living in my building who screams at night. I explained that she keeps me up and now she is saying that I make noise. I chose to tell the truth. I thought it would be good practice for the judge."

"Okay, makes sense. Let's plan to get together for coffee after we leave the courthouse. But I note you said your building, not our building."

"Of course. She doesn't have to know about you."

I laughed.

"Well, I would think she might wonder what kind of noise a single lady like you might make. She might think you would have to be very noisy in order to get summoned."

Sue sighed. "Robert, I told her the lady is a real nut case and that she has no sense of reality. It seemed to satisfy her."

***

The next morning, Sue and I walked over to where we thought might be the best place to catch a taxi. One came screeching to a halt next to where we were standing. We jumped in.

"We are going to the courthouse below Canal Street."

I took the summons out of my jacket pocket and read the taxi driver the address. The cabbie didn't see me read it. He looked in the rear-view mirror after I had put it away.

"There's only one courthouse in this damn city," the cabbie yelled. "Pardon my French, young lady. Are you two going there to get married?"

Sue chuckled, as she gazed out her side window.

"No, neither one of us has popped the question."

The cabbie grunted, "Well, it's none of my business, but if you don't have to get married, don't do it."

He turned his head to look at me.

"I'll tell you why. You lose all your friends! Every damn one of them. They're all out there at the track, or in a poker game, or just having a good old damn time in a saloon. Where are you? Home with the missus watching some lousy TV show. That's where! You look like a smartboy with some 'saichel.' Listen good, young man!"

The cabbie snorted as he wheeled his cab in and out of the traffic.

"No offense to you, young lady."

I ventured with a nod, "We both can't thank you enough for getting us to the courthouse lickety-split. And also, for your sound, 'well thought through advice.' Tell your ex-friends about Lloyd's at 90th Street and 1st Ave. A great saloon for a good old time and best of all, the best roast beef sandwich in the city."

I held Sue's hand as she climbed out of the cab. "We have to find the civil courtroom as soon as we get up the steps. It's only nine-fifteen. We should be fine."

Sue queried, looking quite worried, "What do you think will happen to us?"

I laughed. "I think our old bat neighbor will save our asses. Excuse my French."

Sue furrowed her brow. "How so?"

"The judge. I think it's a magistrate here for civil courts. He will no doubt ask her some questions. Bingo! She will ramble on and he will smell a lunatic. End of story."

"You think?" Sue whispered.

"I think!"

"What did you think about the cabbie's advice? Excuse my French."

"I think he missed his calling. I think he should have been a non-marriage counselor."

We entered the huge hallway which was dimly lit. I thought they might have done better with candles. At the center of the hallway was a man sitting in front of a high brown desk. We approached him and gave him our names. He nodded knowingly and looked in a wine-colored decrepit file.

"Aha! You are to report to the courtroom on the third floor. Room 3C. Hurry now. His honor, the magistrate, does not look fondly on late arrivals."

We turned and headed for the elevator. I held the door for two older gentlemen and Sue. Sue and I squirmed into the elevator, pretty much together. The elevator barely seemed to be moving. It seemed to groan from old age. The more elderly looking of the two gentlemen smiled at Sue.

"You look like a lovely Irish lassie, with that beautiful red hair and all. I hope you know what you are doing, young lady. You know most guys are a bad lot."

He then turned his attention to me and frowned. "Lucky fella. Now treat her good, or I'll be after you." He banged his cane loudly on the floor.

When it finally arrived on the third floor, we quickly exited the elevator. Fortunately for me, they stayed on the elevator. If they were magistrates, they would not be ours. Thank goodness!

We found 3C quickly. We entered the room and a man, about fortyish rushed over to us.

He announced, "I'm a lawyer. No one should go in front of Magistrate Nolan without a lawyer!"

"We'll take our chances, but thanks anyway."

A tall, well-dressed gentleman walked over to us and asked our names. He then ushered us over to a large black table where there were two chairs. I looked to my right.

Yikes! She's there.

She was also sitting behind a large black table. There was only one chair. Hers! I nudged Sue and pointed.

Sue grunted, "I already saw the witch."

In front, to my left, was a woman typing away. I assumed she was the court recorder.

"ALL RISE. HIS HONOR THE MAGISTRATE NOLAN HAS ENTERED THE COURTROOM."

For the first time it hit me. I should be very nervous, and I was very nervous. I looked over at Sue. She looked calm, calm as could be. She obviously believed me. I wished that I did.

For the first time I heard the poor woman's name as the magistrate addressed her.

"Would the plaintiff, Mrs. Florence Gallup, please stand."

The same gentleman, who had taken us to our

chairs, strode up behind the old woman. He nudged her and whispered something in her ear. She slowly rose. She was clearly in physical pain.

"You have filed a complaint against these two defendants. Please tell us your complaint. However, before you do, please swear to tell the truth, the whole truth and nothing but the truth."

"Your honor, these two wild neighbors of mine run up and down the stairs like wild Indians almost every night. Their footsteps are very loud, and it disturbs me."

She then continued on, rambling incoherently. The magistrate looked at her sympathetically.

He addressed the same gentleman, instructing, "Please help remove Mrs. Gallup from this courtroom. I believe she is suffering from hypertension and perhaps delusions."

The magistrate then cast his eyes towards Sue and me.

"Please come forward to my bench."

He narrowed his eyes as we approached. His gaze turned almost completely towards Sue.

"Do you know what you are doing, Miss Cassidy? I suspect there is some hanky-panky going on."

He then turned his gaze on me.

"Tell me, young man, about the physical layout of your two apartments."

"Yes, sir. Miss Cassidy lives directly over me. She lives on the fourth floor. I live on the third floor."

"Did you two ever think that if you got married, how much money you'd save living in the same apartment and sharing the same food?"

The magistrate was shaking his head.

"You young people don't know what's good for you! You are free to go. I dismiss the case. Good luck."

He looked us both over carefully. He seemed sad.

Sue and I hustled over to the elevator. We were alone as we got on. I put my arm around her and turned her toward me.

"That's the second person to look at you and ask, 'Do you know what you are doing?' Do I look that awful? What the hell do they see that you don't?"

"Silly, it's got nothing to do with you. They see me as a young girl, maybe the same age as their daughters. They surmise we are sleeping together out of wedlock. You know very well their generation doesn't approve."

"I guess I'm paranoid about being Jewish. Both those guys seemed Irish to me. I thought they thought you were Irish and shouldn't be messing with a Jewish person."

"Jewish, Schmuish," Sue whispered. "You think too much about being Jewish! Where do you want to go for breakfast? I'm starving!"

Sue held her stomach as the elevator door opened.

I directed, "Let's go back uptown to the Madison. It's late. Most people will have eaten and left. It will be nice and quiet. We'll be able to talk."

"Oh, Oh! Now I'm really getting nervous."

Sue paused and pulled her hair back off her face.

"What do we have to talk about except scrambled eggs, bacon, and the next time that I'll stomp?"

Once I gave the address, everybody was quiet on the ride uptown . . . even the cabbie.

We were sitting across from each other. The Madison restaurant was close to empty. This would be perfect for what I had to tell Sue. I looked straight into her anxiously awaiting blue eyes.

"I quit my day job. I have three more weeks left on my lease on 85th Street. I found an apartment on West 88th Street."

Sue slapped the table.

"You what? You what?? Quit your job? And you're moving? When was I going to hear this news? Am I the last to know?"

Sue frowned.

"Actually, you are the first to know. The only other people that know this are the two landlords and my boss at the day job. Believe me, Sue, it killed me to face having to move. Once I quit my day job that I hated, I had to give up 85th Street. I just couldn't afford it anymore."

"What about us?" Sue exclaimed.

I took a deep breath and urged, "Let's order. The

waitress is heading over to our table."

Sue looked up at the waitress. She forced a smile.

"I'll just have rye toast underneath two poached eggs."

Sue looked back at me. Her eyes were sad. I looked away from Sue. I looked up at the waitress.

"I'll have a cheddar cheese omelet with tomatoes. I'll also have a grilled bialy."

Cheddar cheese is fine in an omelet. Swiss cheese is even fine with Corned Beef. But on roast beef? I don't think so. Cheese has to know its place!

Sue had stayed focused.

"I thought what we were sharing was just perfect."

Sue touched my hand with her finger.

"What's the calamity here? I'm just going a few blocks cross town. It's about a fifteen-minute walk. There are cross-town buses every ten minutes. C'mon, it's not that we are breaking up."

"No?" Sue cried. "It will never be the same! It was the best of the best! When we wanted privacy, we had privacy. We had love making when we wanted it. Not that I intend to move, but what floor are you on in your new place? Is there a floor above you?"

I sadly noted, "Actually, it's a fourth-floor walk-up. I'm on the top floor."

"I knew I should never have encouraged you to make use of your cooking skills. It gives me another reason to hate those damn stinking bars."

Sue looked down at her eggs that had just been placed in front of her. She smiled at the waitress.

"They look great. Thanks."

My omelet also looked delicious. We started to eat.

Sue looked over at me. "By the way, what the hell is a bialy?"

"It's pretty much a bagel without the hole. Mostly they come with a touch of onion. Here, take a bite."

I held the bialy close to Sue.

"No thanks. I have a late flight tonight. The last thing I need today is onion breath. I just want you to know, Robert, I'm not happy about what you are doing. And I'm definitely not climbing up on your roof on West 88th Street and stomping."

Sue laughed. At last, the shine had returned to those beautiful blue eyes.

I placed my hand on Sue's arm. "You'll see. We'll still be okay. We'll be fine. Let's head back to the apartment. I need to figure out what to take and what not to take."

"Well, I'm not going to help you move!" Sue stated firmly as she slid off her chair.

She tucked her little finger under my chin. "I should stay angry with you, but I won't." She headed out the door.

22

ABBIE IS RELENTLESS

WHEN I GOT back to my place, I started going through some of my pants pockets. In one of them, I found a few crumpled dollars. In another, I found the piece of paper Diane handed me at the Simon and Garfunkel concert. I couldn't believe what I saw. Not only did it have her phone number, but it had her address. It was West 88th Street, two doors up from my new place.

I'd go over to Lloyd's. I'd cook up a couple of roast beefs for Lloyd's and Brandy's too.

As I came in, the jukebox was blaring *My Boyfriend's Back*. I headed to the kitchen. Charlie came in.

"I don't see the vodka bottle that I put here."

He grunted. His hand seemed knotted as if he were making a fist.

"Charlie, it must be here somewhere. I'll look for it later. Things can get pretty messy around here. Mostly because we make sandwiches as quickly as possible. I'll also ask Jake if he's seen it."

I tried to clear off the counter.

"Remember, I told you to guard it with your life. I wasn't kidding!" Charlie snarled and walked back toward the bar.

The day went along well.

Natasha was smiling when she advised, "Abbie Hoffman is back at The Table."

The jukebox was playing *Blowin' in the Wind*. Abbie had gotten up to play it. He was smiling. He turned his gaze over towards Charlie.

I walked over to The Table. Abbie pointed at the chair next to him for me to sit down. He placed his hand on my shoulder and pulled me closer to him.

"Have you thought about what I presented to you the last time I was here?"

I lied, "Of course."

"You seemed worried about money. There will be no need for money in the world that I and my followers will create. We hate money. We hate that so few have it, and so many don't. I'm thinking of writing a book. The cover and title will read, *Steal This Book*. I can only wonder if they will publish a book with that title. But no need to worry about money. You won't need money ever again! Join us in our fight against the establishment."

"Abbie, I really appreciate your invite, but I have to refuse. I'm just getting started here. I need to give myself a chance."

"You are totally out of the real picture! I just played *Blowin' in the Wind* by Peter, Paul and Mary. Sure, they have good voices. Sure, they harmonize well together. But their interpretation sucks. They really don't get the words. Not really! More than likely the real version is being sung right at this moment by the incredible songwriter, Mr. Bob Dylan down in the village. That's where it's happening! Not here!"

Abbie shifted to a low confidential monotone. "The place is The Bitter End. It's not Lloyd's. Tonight, I'll bet Dylan will sing, *The Times They Are a Changin'* Robert, have you heard that song? Are you hip to the lyrics? That's our national anthem!"

Now Abbie glared at me. The challenge in his eyes was as electric and powerful as his smile had been.

"Yes, of course, I've heard it. Who hasn't?"

Abbie leaned in closer. "Robert, this place is the epitome of APATHY. Talk about *apathy*! A few months ago, a woman named Kitty Genovese was murdered. It was reported that thirty-seven neighbors witnessed the stabbing. She was stabbed at least seventeen times and raped, while people watched. Robert, they WATCHED.

They just WATCHED!!" Abbie pointed at his eyes. "Lloyd's makes me think of that killing. I look around and no one seems to care what's really going on. They just seem concerned about what they are drinking and who they might get to fuck tonight."

Abbie stretched his arms on The Table and pushed himself up. "Jerry Rubin and I will be heading south in just six days. Some guys and girls will be joining us. We'll probably be about twenty or so to start, at least with my group. Sorry you won't be with us. I'm sure you will regret your decision for the rest of your life. That's how important I believe this cause is. I'm willing to wager that a ton of books will be written about this. Movies will be made, but they will be bullshit. They will only be produced to sell tickets. They really won't get it. When we get done, you'll be looking at a very different world."

Abbie walked over to the jukebox and played *We Shall Overcome*. He concentrated his gaze on Charlie as he made his exit.

23

THE GIRLS THAT STUFFED

ARE BACK

AS I GOT up to get back to the kitchen, some psychic person played *Breaking Up Is Hard to Do*. I looked over to see who it was. There were Lois and Sandy. I hadn't seen Lois or Sandy since they had helped so much in the beginning of this business. I don't believe I ever thanked them enough for stuffing my ads into mailboxes. Lois was heading back to her table where Sandy was sitting. Finally, we'll connect again. Lois spotted me. She smiled and motioned with both her arms for me to join them.

"We've missed you," they seemed to say in unison.

Lois elaborated, "I'm celebrating my break-up with my former boyfriend. We had a huge argument last night. One of the reasons you haven't seen me, or even either of us, here much has been because of my boyfriend. He doesn't like bars."

Lois was biting her lip. It looked like it hurt.

Sandy piped up, "I don't have any excuses. I just don't like coming into bars by myself. I'm still seeing that talkative Jewish guy. Nothing serious, at least not yet."

I pointed at the kitchen. "Can I bring you some food? It's on the house, or should I say that it's on the kitchen!"

"You owe us at least that."

Lois smiled like a Cheshire cat and continued, "We were actually talking about how you could repay us for all those fliers we stuffed. We were talking about a sexual Pepsi challenge. The reason is both of us have slept with this handsome window salesman that comes in here a lot. We frequently ask him to tell us who he thinks is better in bed, but he refuses to rate us. All we get is that it depends on the bed."

"So what am I being asked here? Please tell this very naïve Boston transplant where I come in? Please excuse my phrasing."

"Well, besides the sandwiches we are hungering for, we both want you to sleep with us. After you do, we want to be rated."

Now Lois twinkled as her smile widened. She

seemed excited. She was no longer biting her lip.

"On a scale of zero to ten, or zero to one-hundred?" I pondered. "And do I get rated as well?"

Lois looked over at me. "No, not numbers. We want to be rated as follows: Fair, Not bad, Good, Excellent, Very Recommendable. As far as rating you, your job is just to get down to business, shut the hell up, and follow our instructions! If you do all that, you'll be fine."

Sandy raised her eyebrows. "There won't be any need to grade you."

I offered enthusiastically, "I'm leaving 85th Street in two weeks. I'd suggest, as you say, we get down to business in the next couple of days. In fact, why not tomorrow night? For whoever wants firsties."

Lois jumped up. "We already flipped. I won!"

I pointed at my watch. "And can you be at my apartment at 10:30 tomorrow night?"

Lois was beaming.

"Yes! I'll be there at 10:28 sharp, if you get my meaning," Lois crooned, as she added, "without a lot of clothes on."

Sandy purred, "I can be there Tuesday evening at 10:30. Does that work okay for you?"

"Yup, I may even get there early! But FIRST, what do you want to eat NOW?"

"We'll have two of your juiciest, thickest sandwiches, no onion and plenty of your dressing shmeared on both sides of the rolls."

Once again, they seemed to be speaking together.

I grinned. "Fulfillment of all of your requests coming right up!!"

***

The next evening, I was preparing a few sandwiches for Natasha. As she came over, I asked her if she knew who the gentleman sitting at The Table was.

Natasha looked puzzled. "No! I never saw him before. He ordered two sandwiches and asked me if I could tell him who Robert is. I was about to tell you that someone was looking for you. He didn't give me his name, but I sat him at The Table, because he was asking for you."

I had intended to say hello to Skip who had just come in, but instead I walked over to The Table feeling as puzzled as the look on Natasha's face. The gentleman stood up, smiled and put his hand out for me to shake.

"My name is Steve Foreman. I've been hearing about your sandwiches. I've seen your ads. What a wonderful counterpoint to Prexy's ads for 'Hamburgers with a College Education' when you promote 'Our Sandwiches Are Not Only Illiterate, They're Thick!' Your waitress is about to bring me over two of them."

I reached over and shook his hand. I sat down across from him, wondering what he wanted and why.

I opened with, "Nice to meet you."

"You as well. It's great to be in the presence of the 'Fairly Famous' Robert."

Natasha arrived with a sly smile. She half turned, as she placed the sandwiches carefully in the center of The Table. They were perfectly warm. Steve took a hearty bite. "Yum, double yum! Best roast beef sandwich I've ever tasted. Matter of fact, maybe the best sandwich I've ever tried."

"Thanks very much. I'm very pleased that you've heard about them. I'm even more pleased that you like them."

Steve looked unflinchingly into my eyes. "Yes, I came here to ask you a question that could change your life forever."

"Yeah? What's the question?"

"Have you ever heard of franchising?" "Yes, but I don't know much about it."

Steve nodded. "Well, I do know a lot about franchising. I'd like to franchise your amazing product."

"That's a lot to digest. Let me think about it. Give me two days. I'll have an answer for you then."

I put out my hand towards Steve. He placed one hand on my shoulder and met my handshake with a powerful, almost painful grip. As I walked over to Skip, I ducked into the kitchen and picked up my half-finished drink that I had left behind. The jukebox was blaring *The Wanderer*.

"Hey, Skip, haven't seen you in a while. Where have you been?"

Skip laughed. "I've been very busy with Yanna.

Remember her, the yoga fanatic? Let me put it this way, she doesn't have me doing yoga. I also made a date with that Daryl I told you about. It's for next Wednesday. I'm excited. It's as if I were a little kid."

"It sounds like you are keeping busy. It all sounds good."

I fumbled with the almost empty glass.

"I've got a dilemma. Did you notice the guy I was just talking to? He loves my business. Well, maybe not my business per se, he likes the sandwiches. He wants me to leave here and start roast beef franchises."

"You can't leave! We'll all starve to death! You have helped turn this place around," Skip enthused as he placed his hand tightly on my shoulder. "We are getting a better class of women in here because of your sandwiches."

His voice was rising. "YOU CAN'T LEAVE!"

"I feel so torn. My dad wants me to come back to Boston. Sue is upset that I'm moving to the West Side. Who the hell knows where I'd have to go if I say yes to this franchise guy?"

With a big grin, Skip offered, "Let me buy you another one of those drinks you drink. Your drink looks thirsty. That will calm you down and set you straight!"

"Maybe, but another drink won't change things. I know because I've been drinking all evening."

I took another sip. It made that gurgling sound Charlie had mentioned he loathed. "Anyhow, thanks very much for the offer and the kind compliments for the food. I've got to meet someone soon. Say hello to Dick when you see him."

It was starting to approach ten o'clock. I thought I'd tell Natasha I'd leave a little early tonight and early tomorrow night. I wanted to get my place neatened up tonight so it would be ready for Lois tomorrow night. This was very different from any previous experience I'd had. This was an *all the cards on the table* occasion. No small talk required. No talk of a "famous pasta recipe" that Sue had invited me to before we made love. Still, I was nervous. I would have to measure up. Pardon the pun, I thought to myself. Lois had told me she was sleeping with that cool-looking Italian window salesman. Lois had also mentioned that she had broken up with her boyfriend. Sleeping with two different guys on different nights, it seemed Lois must be very experienced. But, I thought, I'd just have to hold my own. Once again, I yelled at my insidious brain to stop the bad puns.

***

That night, I cleaned up as well as I could. The next day passed quickly. Then I lay down on the bed and waited for Lois as patiently as possible. For no good reason, I remembered the blind dates I had gone on back in Dorchester. I had tried to make insipid conversation with my dates, asking if they had seen "From Here to Eternity?", "Did they like Elvis?" Nothing I did ever worked. I was always groping for something to say and never finding the right words. Am I the same guy having Lois come to my place and honoring me with her body? I won't even have to ask her if she likes Bob Dylan's new recording!

The doorbell rang. I got off the bed and buzzed her up. I opened the door so that it was just ajar. then I went back to my bed. Lois came bursting through the door and practically flew next to me on the bed.

"I'm so excited to be back in your apartment for some fun and games! The last time I was here, I was given a bunch of flyers to stuff."

Lois's enthusiasm was catchy! I nodded. "Fun and games! I'll start."

I got up and began undressing. Lois lay on the bed, staring at my every move. After all my clothes were off, Lois smiled and remarked, "You'll do."

At least she didn't comment 'You'll have to do.'

Lois rose from the bed. She began stripping, doing a little dance as each piece of clothing came off. Lois was shorter than either Pat or Sue. She was also rounder, but still delicious looking. Finally, when all her clothes were off, she jumped back on the bed.

Lois sang out, "Let's get started."

When we finished, Lois, who had moaned a lot, started talking about her two other lovers.

Lois informed me, "Anthony can't wait to finish. It's like he has a time limit. But even though he's what us girls call a minute-man, he's kind and always asks how it was for me. I never know what to say. My ex is very slow and methodical. Sexually he's a delight."

I grinned as I touched her thigh.

"Do you know how many times you let out an 'Oh Jesus!' I wasn't counting, but a lot. Sometimes it was 'Jesus Christ!' . . . and one time 'Jesus H. Christ.' I found it very inspiring and exciting. So much so it even made me think of converting. I was just wondering what you would scream next. You also uttered 'G-D damn! Fuck me!' towards our finale."

Lois asked hesitantly, "Anyway, I came here for a rating. What do you give me?"

"The best!" I exclaimed. "It was terrific. If someone asked me, I would definitely say how good it was with you."

I moved my hand to her naked breast. She placed her hand on top of mine.

Lois sighed and went on, "Well, should anyone ask, let me know. Thank you, I'll do my own screening. Before I leave, I'd like to shower. Is that okay?"

"Hey, take your shower, I'll grab a towel and dry you," I proposed.

Lois smiled. "In that case I'm going to get very wet."

She took my hand from her breasts and moved off the bed.

Lois headed for the bathroom and came out dripping wet.

"After I get dressed, I'm going to head home. Will

you walk out with me and help get me a taxi?"

I nodded. "Of course. Your call. You are welcome to stay the night, but it shouldn't be a problem getting a cab at this hour."

I bent over and tossed her pink panties to her outstretched hands. I thought about the little dance she had done when she took her panties off. Lois reached out and grabbed them.

"I'll come back for seconds whenever it's good for you." Lois laughed as she spoke, "Talk about stuffing mailboxes, I finally got my money's worth. You paid me back in full. Not bad for a Boston boy."

We flagged down a cab almost as soon as we walked out the door. It was that time of night. I held the door for Lois and bent over to give her a goodnight kiss and added, "Great night, pretty girl!"

I smiled as the cab roared off.

24

THE FRANCHISE PROPOSAL

THE NEXT EVENING was going to be interesting. I would be entertaining Sandy at about 10:30. The franchise guy was coming for my answer. I remembered we hadn't set a time, but my guess was he'd come about the same time as he had before, about 8'ish.

What the hell was I going to say? I knew nothing about franchising. What would I bring along to a franchise business? Here at Lloyd's, I had something going. I hadn't really taken full advantage of my situation. Women were streaming in, night after night. Tonight, I'd be with Sandy. Last night, Lois. This was just a tip of the iceberg. Girls liked being fed, especially if the food was as good as what I was serving. More and more of them would take notice of the chef. There—I declared it. Chef, not cook! Pretty soon I'd be making some serious money. Lloyd's was picking up each night as the word got out about the sandwiches. Brandy's was going to expand. Arnie was planning that 'Robert's Fairly Famous' would be part of the whole shebang. What did I know about the franchise guy? Nothing! Here at Lloyd's I was mostly my own boss, except every once in a while, Charlie had something to say to me. But fortunately, that was only once in a while.

I was also pretty certain Sue was right. It could never be the same with me going to the West Side. Of course Sue wasn't going to move to the West Side. She was only joking when she asked what floor I was on. Even if she wasn't kidding, I would never be able to hear stomps from a rooftop. Maybe I should take both Abbie's and Charlie's advice. The more the merrier. I'm too young, too poor, to consider a real serious relationship leading to marriage. What did Bruce Jay Friedman's book advise, right on the cover . . . *Sleep 'til Noon and Screw Them All!?*

The other evening as I walked by the bar, I heard a fellow say to his buddy, tapping him on the noggin, "*No*, means *Yes*. Never, ever believe in *No*. You should have been removing her blouse on the second *No.*" He paused for a second, "This is the Sixties! Girls want it even more than we do. They're all on the pill. The Fifties, my friend, are long gone. You can thank your lucky stars for that."

His buddy was nodding his thanks for the enlightenment. "I get it! Next time I'll know better and I'll do better!"

What the hell was I thinking? I always thought *No* meant *No*. Anyway, I never even got as far as a *No* back in Dorchester. Here, in the city, I haven't had to ask. I've been more than fortunate. I already knew I'd be terrible at asking. Maybe that guy is right, but I knew *no* would always mean *no* to me. I was not an interpreter.

Natasha strolled over to me. She cupped her hands over her mouth. "That guy is back. I sat him down at The Table. He ordered two more sandwiches, a 'Robert's' salad and coleslaw. I guess he is planning to be here a while."

The jukebox was playing *Duke of Earl*. Some women were up swaying to the song. They seemed to be laughing every time Gene Chandler sang the words "I'm the Duke of Earl."

Natasha pointed to an expensive-looking, shiny leather briefcase under the table. "I also noted that he had a briefcase. He didn't have one the last time he came."

I quickly made up his order and handed it to Natasha. I grabbed a napkin from the kitchen counter and stuck it in my pocket. I began a slow walk to The Table. The jukebox was now playing *Blue Velvet*.

Steve welcomed me, "Sit, sit down."

Steve smiled as he held up one of the sandwiches,

Natasha had brought him.

"Get comfortable."

Steve indicated the chair opposite him. His head was nodding again.

"Robert, I'm ready to get started. How about you?"

He bit into the sandwich. As he chewed, he brought the briefcase up on The Table. Steve looked into my eyes.

I met his gaze. "I've been thinking ever since we talked two days ago. I have to say no."

"Robert, I believe you are making the mistake of a lifetime. You have a fantastic product and a great name. We could make some hay together."

Steve began to eat his salad.

He continued, "Hope I'm not being impolite by eating while we are speaking, but your food is so damn good. I just can't resist it."

"Go right ahead! Eat and enjoy. That is why I cook. I want *eaters* to eat."

I paused and then tried to explain, "I've spent the last couple of days thinking about your offer. I have reasons for turning you down. I've worked the last few months at getting 'Robert's Fairly Famous' off the ground. I started this whole thing in my apartment over on 85th Street. I'm just getting it out there now, supplying food to two bars. I believe there are more bars to come. I want to give this fledgling idea a chance to work. It needs to breathe and grow naturally. I believe to push it out widely now would be a mistake for me."

I watched Steve chewing on his sandwich with great delight, but his eyes looked very puzzled.

"Robert, you are making the mistake of a lifetime. Lloyd's and the other place are not where it's at. I'm talking—the country with franchises. Maybe the world!"

Steve was breathing heavily now.

"Well, perhaps I'll live to regret this decision, but I'll live with it, good or bad."

I used the napkin I thought I had brought for him, to wipe my own forehead.

Steve pushed The Table toward me. He had finished all his food.

"Robert, it was very nice to meet you. I wish you the best. I'm truly sorry that it is 'no.'"

"Great to meet you too, Steve. I really appreciate your offer. I very much appreciate your coming back to talk to me."

As at our last encounter, he reached out to my extended hand. I recalled his very firm grip. I walked away from The Table thinking that I should have asked a lot of questions. But the truth was I really didn't want answers. The truth was I was scared to death to make another move.

I went back to the kitchen. Connie Francis was singing, *Who's Sorry Now*. Was that an omen?

25

SANDY AND I CUT A DEAL

THE REST OF the evening went smoothly. We sold about fifty-five sandwiches and a ton of potato salad. I had lost count as I wondered why the potato salad had suddenly taken off.

Natasha came into the kitchen. "Good night so far. I know you want to leave early. Have you got another hot one tonight?"

Natasha smirked as I nodded. "Yes, I appreciate you covering for me. I'll see you tomorrow. You can give me the count then. By the way, how have the tips been?"

Natasha was almost screaming, "NEVER ENOUGH! Now get out of here! Out of my sight! And remember to fully appreciate the woman, whoever she might be. She might be somebody's mother one day."

Natasha looked delighted as she offered me this advice. I scampered out and made it to my apartment in no time at all. I was glad Sue would have some overnights in other cities, as in last night and tonight. Perfect! I'd get ready for Sandy. I opened a bottle of white wine and put some crackers in a bowl next to a cheese dip. I neatened up as best I could and lay down on the bed, exactly as I had done waiting for Lois.

The doorbell rang and I buzzed Sandy up. She knocked on the door that I hadn't opened. She was standing there, wearing a violet dress underneath a white angora sweater. She looked dressed for a date.

I smiled. "Hello! Great to see you."

"Likewise."

Sandy brushed by me. She pulled a chair out and faced it toward my bed. Sandy pointed at my bed and gestured for me to sit down. I grabbed the bowl of crackers and dip, placed it near me and Sandy on the bed, close enough for Sandy to help herself without having to stretch.

"Robert, I'm not sure I like what we are doing. I don't want to be in a sex contest with Lois. I like you, Robert. I like you a lot. I like what you have accomplished in a short time." Sandy sighed as she awaited my response.

"Thanks a lot. I really appreciate your words. I don't often hear them from my own head. My head plays a different tune."

I tapped my head as if to scold it. Sandy smiled.

"You are only twenty-three and you have started your own business. You should be very proud of yourself. I know I am proud of you. But I don't want a one-night stand. I want more. I want to know you. I want to get to like you better than I already do and that's a lot." Sandy reached over and took a couple of crackers.

"Wow! So many compliments."

I grabbed a handful of crackers, paused, and then confessed, "Actually, all of the accomplishments, if there are any, are a result of not liking my day job."

Sandy looked at me. "Do you still want to have my body, after that speech?" She then touched her lips as she offered, "No ties either way."

"I think we should keep things as they are. Let's stay friends. Maybe some other time after we get to know each other better, perhaps then we'll enjoy each other's bodies even more."

I leaned over and touched Sandy's knee.

Sandy whispered, "I'd like to sleep in your bed tonight even if we don't have sex."

"Sounds like a plan. I'd say a great start in getting to know one another better."

I kicked off my shoes.

***

When I awakened the next morning, Sandy was hugging me as she slept. I got out of bed as gently as I could and tried my best not to disturb her. I stumbled to the bathroom where I brushed my teeth, gargled, took a hurried shower and started to put on some outdoor clothes. Sandy rose, blinking her eyes. She smiled.

"Are you going somewhere? You are all dressed. By the way, by chance, do you have an extra toothbrush? May I shower before I leave?"

"Of course you can shower, but I'm not going out just yet. I'm going to eat something. You and Lois have a lot in common. She also showered here before she left. And yes, I've got a drawer full of unused toothbrushes . . . top drawer on the right."

"Tell you what! Don't fix yourself any breakfast. I know a great coffee shop around the corner. My treat. I want to celebrate our first night together."

Sandy pulled at her messed up hair. She headed for the bathroom to find a toothbrush and shower.

Just as I was about to say yes, that it was a great idea to go out for breakfast, the phone rang. It was Jake.

"I need to meet you for breakfast. We need to talk."

Jake sounded concerned.

"Where and what time?"

"My favorite breakfast place near you is The Madison Café. Do you know where it is?"

"Yeah, I just had breakfast there with Sue after the magistrate dismissed the case."

I tightened my belt.

"Oh yeah, I want to hear all about that. It's also important that we talk this morning. I've got a couple of things on my mind. How is ten o'clock?"

I agreed, "Perfect. I'll be there at ten."

I turned to Sandy, who was coming out of the shower with a towel wrapped around her.

"Can't make breakfast this morning. But thanks very much for the offer. I'll see you at Lloyd's and we'll make another date."

"Shit! I was looking forward to sitting across from you. I was hoping that we could get to know each other. You and I both know it can't happen at Lloyd's."

Sandy tightened the towel as she added, "Oh well. Lloyd's it will have to be."

"Thanks for understanding. You remember Jake? You met him here. He passed out the flyers and set up the streets you guys covered. Anyway, he just called. He's worried about something. Maybe it's about Lloyd's. In any case, he's been terrific. I have to scram. Please close the door very tightly when you leave. It's one of those troublesome doors."

Sandy nodded and laughed. "Will do, sir."

She saluted me. Her mouth tasted fresh as I gave her a kiss goodbye. I smiled to myself. I always had extra toothbrushes.

I hurried down to the Madison. Jake was already sitting at a table, sipping on what was probably tea. Jake had a way of saying "Tea" whenever a waitress would offer him coffee. It was like the waiter or waitress should know by looking at Jake that he was a man of taste. He wouldn't stoop to coffee when he could have "Tea."

Jake looked concerned.

"Sit. We need to talk. I'm glad you could make it here. First off, I need you to cover for me Sunday. A bunch of us, mostly Brandeis Alum, will be having a goodbye party for Abbie. Ira invited you as well, but many of the people that will be there are people that I went to school with. I'm really looking forward to seeing and talking with them again."

"I understand. Anyway, Abbie would probably buttonhole me again about going with SDS to who knows where down south. I've already told him 'no' twice. But I will want to hear all about the party. Blow by blow! Call me next week and fill me in. Pardon the pun, but we both know how Abbie likes to brag about getting the BEST head in the city. Anyway, you've got more to tell me. Shoot."

"Yuh, I do." Jake squirmed in his chair. "Charlie has been acting strangely. It was even more noticeable last Sunday. He kept coming into the kitchen. He kept picking things up, and pushing stuff around. Finally, he shouted, 'Where's that fuckin' vodka bottle?' Of course, I didn't know what to say."

Jake sat up in his chair and leaned towards me.

"You know I don't remember noticing that bottle, even after you told me Charlie insisted that you guard it with your life. Also, Gloria came in a little later and she asked for a 'Robert's Fairly Famous' salad. I brought it to her. She took a very small bite and asked, 'What is the salad dressing made up of?' She picked up the dish. She actually seemed to be sniffing it. I told her the ingredients that you told me to use for her. She looked at me with disbelief in her eyes."

I pondered, "What does she think? That we're trying to poison her? You know, I've got to tell you what Arnie from Brandy's suggested about Charlie."

Jake interrupted, "She indicated something about her strict diet." Jake sipped his tea. "Something like she hoped 'Robert's' dressing wouldn't be a dietary problem for her."

I grimaced.

"The salad dressing caper? Sounds like a bad movie! Anyway, Arnie heard from the bar gossip board that Charlie was a 'character.' He's a very jealous and paranoid person. Sooner or later we'd get thrown out like all the other previous cooks."

Jake stirred more sugar into his tea as he spoke, "Actually, until last Sunday, Charlie and I have had what I thought was a good relationship. I have to admit after watching him messing in the kitchen, I wasn't so sure. I did hear from Ira that Abbie stopped by Lloyd's a few days ago. Ira told me Abbie described Charlie as bad news. There had been some very ugly eye contact between Abbie and Charlie."

The waitress came over with a question and an

offer.

"What will you two boys have? It's already ten-thirty. You can still have breakfast or lunch. We are open for either now."

Jake looked up.

"I'll have an omelet very well done with a sliced tomato inside the omelet."

"Make that two, but I'll also have onions and peppers in the omelet's innards."

The waitress smiled. "Coming right up. Just sit tight. I'll have your grub here in no time." She paused, as she looked over at Jake. "Do you need any more hot water for that tea of yours?"

Jake shifted in his chair. "No, I'm fine for now."

The waitress walked off to the kitchen.

Jake looked up at me and whispered, "I felt like leaving when she called our food 'grub.'"

"We've got more serious problems than that. The answer about Sunday is definitely 'yes.' I'm looking forward to checking out the Sunday crowd. Maybe Charlie will be there Sunday. If he is, I'll try to talk to him."

The waitress brought our plates. She looked over at Jake.

"I hope it's well done enough for you."

Jake countered with a friendly wink at the waitress. "So do I."

The waitress nodded at Jake. She then turned to me and smirked.

"I hope you enjoy the innards."

I finished my food quickly and noted that Jake was not yet even half finished.

"I've got to take off. Don't forget you've got to tell me all the lurid party details."

I placed a five-dollar bill on the table.

"That should be more than enough to cover our breakfast. Thanks for the heads-up about Charlie and Gloria. Also, we never got to talk about what happened in court. When we speak next, I'll elaborate."

26

THE PROFESSOR

TEACHES ME SAICHEL

SUNDAY CAME AS it always does, at the end of the week or the beginning of a new week. I guess it depends on whether you're a half-empty or half-full kind of guy. I got to Lloyd's at about 11:30 a.m. George was the bartender. The only two patrons were the Professor and his buddy. I was pretty sure the Professor's name was Ernest. I was certain he taught a sociology course at either N.Y.U. or the New School for Social Research or both!

I decided to go over to talk to them before I went

into the kitchen.

"Hi, I'm Robert."

The Professor swiveled his bar stool around to face me.

"We know who you are. We really like your food. All of it! What an improvement you have made here. Keep it up for our sakes."

The Professor nudged his buddy who nodded his agreement.

"Thanks, I really appreciate you gentlemen saying such nice things."

I thrust out my hand to shake theirs. The Professor waved off my handshake. He smiled.

"We were having one of our usual arguments. My buddy Phil here, likes to call them 'discussions.' We were 'discussing.'"

The Professor looked at Phil for approval of his word usage.

"Yes, we were speculating on who would be the mightiest world power in the next century."

The Professor took out a thin stogie and was contemplating it.

I chimed in, "That's a long way away."

The Professor put a long hard stare on me, "Who would you say will be the world's leader fifty or sixty years from now?"

He lit his very thin stogie.

I laughed. "I just hope whoever they are that they will still be eating my roast beef sandwiches."

They both laughed as well.

"Phil here thinks it will be the Japanese, with India coming in a strong second. As usual, I say Phil is dead wrong."

Phil laughed. Actually, it was much more of a snort than a laugh.

The Professor declared, "I say positively it will be China! No question! They have the manpower, but most of all they have the *'saichel.'* You know what *'saichel'* is don't you Robert?"

The Professor leaned towards me. I nodded.

"Yuh, I do. It's Jewish for smarts."

The Professor, Ernest, wasn't finished yet.

"I'm not Jewish, but I'm a great admirer of the Jewish people and their endurance and longevity. As a matter of fact, I intend to write a book about the Jewish people. I already have a title for it. Something along the lines of The Jewish Mystique, but please don't mention it to anyone yet."

"Exciting. I'll buy it for sure or maybe I could trade a few roast beef sandwiches for the book. I want to know more about the Jewish people, especially from a non- Jewish perspective."

"You see the Chinese people have a quality that is very rare in this world. It's called patience."

The Professor puffed on his stogie exhaling very deliberately.

"The Chinese had to learn it the hard way. But learn

it they did. And now they practice it."

He snuffed out his stogie very carefully in the ashtray.

"Patience, young man. Patience!"

The Professor tapped his buddy Phil on the shoulder as he finished speaking.

I spoke up, "Can I get you two any lunch?"

"Yes, bring us four of your juiciest. We'll be sitting at that table over there."

Ernest pointed to the table furthest from the kitchen, but near the jukebox, which was suddenly playing *I Want to Hold Your Hand* by The Beatles.

While I had been talking to the Professor and Phil, a young couple had come into Lloyd's. They were standing in front of the jukebox and giggling. They were holding hands.

Phil pointed at the table that Ernest requested.

"Yuh, we have two young lovelies meeting us here in about fifteen minutes."

Phil licked his lips.

"Bring us four coleslaws as well. Believe me, if I have to kick the Professor, we'll lighten up the conversation."

I went back to the kitchen feeling pretty okay about my decision not to go with the franchise guy. Where else could I meet and talk to such interesting people? Not many places I thought, but I knew that I would always wonder what I had missed.

Natasha came wandering in. She looked like she had an interesting night after she left Lloyd's.

I pointed at the Professor's table and winked. "After you get these sandwiches and coleslaws over to those two guys, tell me all about your night."

Natasha had just delivered the food to Phil and Ernest. She slid herself back into the kitchen and onto the one kitchen chair that we had which was in front of the stove. Natasha took a deep breath.

"You know, you guys are such creeps. Always asking for the gory details. One of the semi-regulars here, his name is Peter. He asked if I'd go to an after-hours club with him. I did. He came home with me and we had marvelous, exotic, perverted sex. Anything to say to that?"

"Not really, except I'm jealous."

"Well, stay jealous, cause that's all you're going to get from me. You know the expression very well, 'You don't shit where you eat.' I'd change it to 'Why screw up a good working relationship?' Note the 'screw up.'"

"Okay, let's shake hands and come out hugging. Besides I didn't ask for anything more. Being jealous is a compliment, that's all. It looks like a slow night. Let's cut out early."

"Sundays are frequently like this. Folks getting ready for Monday. But we did sell forty sandwiches. That's pretty good for a Sunday and quite a few salads."

"Good enough. We'll wind up at about 10:00 tonight." I'd check on what had happened at Brandy's on Monday. There was good reason to get back to my apartment before it got any later. Sue would be home early Sunday evening.

Just as I opened the door to my apartment, the phone was ringing. I hoped it would be Sue. It wasn't. It was Jake.

"You wanted me to call and tell you about the going away party for Abbie. It was everything you could imagine and more. Abbie made his entrance long after the party started. He came in with that incredible smile. You know the one."

"Yeah," I acknowledged a trifle unhappily.

"The place just burst apart. It was like a lightning bolt had shot through the room. The girls started gyrating to the music. A few blouses and bras hit the floor. It was the party to end all parties. Very sorry we both couldn't be there. Maybe when he returns, you'll go, and I'll cover."

Jake was finally finished.

"Okay and thanks for the report. I'm signing off to call Sue. See you soon."

I dialed Sue. "Hello."

"Hello yourself. I thought you took Sundays off. I thought Jake was holding down the Lloyd's fort on Sundays? Both my feet are screaming ouch from stomping so much. I was getting worried about your hearing."

Sue giggled.

"He does and has. But there was a going away party for Abbie. Jake thought he'd see a lot of his Brandeis buddies there."

Sue scolded, "You could have told me. How come you didn't go?"

"We both couldn't be at the party. Someone had to cover Lloyd's."

"Anyway, c'mon up. Maybe you'll pay me back with a foot massage. You know I'm on my feet all week. I'm sure my feet always say 'thank you' when I get a day off. I think they resented all of the stomping I did today."

I could hear Sue's soft ripple of laughter as I scurried up the stairs. Her door was ajar. I was wondering if she'd be naked, as she was the last time that her door was slightly ajar. She wasn't. Sue was fully dressed. She was in the kitchen slicing up a cucumber. "I made us a dip." Sue pointed at a cup.

Sue looked up at me. "I figured we could try to eat a little healthier. We can use the cucumber for dipping, rather than those salty crackers I always put out."

Sue licked some dip off her lips. "I'm glad you're here. We both know that when you move, we won't see each other as much."

"Hey, we've discussed it. I'll try my best to still make it work. I don't get it that you somehow think I don't care as much as you do."

"It's like what I explained a long time ago. I told you that if you and Pat were really serious with each other, you would have gone to Michigan or she would have transferred to a New York college."

Sue continued in a whisper, "Now you are moving to the West Side, because you can't earn enough money in those two stinking bars!"

"That's true, but it keeps growing every day. In fact, a franchise expert wanted to take my 'Robert's Fairly Famous' idea and franchise it."

I dipped a cucumber slice into the dip. Sue looked puzzled.

"So, what happened?"

"I turned him down."

"You what!" Sue exclaimed as she shook a cucumber slice menacingly at me. "You had a chance to get out of those crummy places, with a business yet, and you didn't take it!"

Sue raised her voice even louder.

"Why the hell didn't you tell me? Why the hell didn't you ask me?"

Sue's voice was cracking.

"It all happened pretty fast. You were away. I told him 'no' because I thought I'd be in a business I knew nothing about. I didn't know the man. I felt it was all a foreign language to me. Maybe, I'm just a scaredy cat after all."

I slapped my head.

Sue grew quiet.

"Well, that's a closed case, but I've got some ideas for you."

Sue pushed the dip closer to my plate.

"I've told you about all those wealthy guys that take me out to dinner after a flight. Well, I learn a lot when I'm out with them. Usually they are very bright. These men are focused on what they do for a living."

Sue took a breath.

I spoke up, "Most people are pretty focused on what they do. Aren't you?"

"Maybe if you'd be quiet for a couple of minutes, I can tell you what I'm thinking!"

Sue took another deep breath.

"One cannot talk enough about computers. He says over and over again that this is the time to get into computers. It's the future he claims."

Sue bit into a cucumber slice.

"He says he could recommend companies to start with where the starting pay is reasonable. I have his card." Sue dived into her purse and took out a business card.

She smiled.

"I have a lot of these cards."

"Interesting. Maybe I should check it out."

I gulped the soda Sue had put out.

"That's just one thought. Another one claims it's all

about finance. He says go to where the money rests. He loves to quote Wille Sutton. When people asked Willie why he robbed banks, he always replied, 'That's where the money is.'"

Sue was carrying on like she was on a mission. I'd never seen or heard Sue like this before.

"Robert, you are too smart, too good a person to be going to these bars night after bloody night. You are my best friend. I like you more than anybody else I know. I only want two things from you. Number one: Don't move to the West Side. Number two: Find another job!!"

Sue was red faced. Her fingers were pressing hard against my arm.

"I hear you very clearly, but I want to make this business work."

I touched Sue's fingers.

"You already have. You came here to New York. You only knew one person. Look what you've accomplished. Look at how many people have enjoyed your sandwiches."

I pulled my hand away from Sue.

"So, you are saying I should quit now. I want to make this work on my terms."

I looked straight into Sue's eyes.

"I don't want to have to work for anyone."

I dipped the cucumber slice into the dip.

"The last flight I was on, I met this gentleman who was telling me all about his business. We were coming back from O'Hare in Chicago. He'd been at Sears all day talking to them about his product. He told me that he was a rep for a company in Patterson, New Jersey that makes waterproof boots. I've got his card right here. He's always looking for bright young men to work with him."

Sue held up a card that read Eric J. Metzger and Associates, Inc.

"Note he wants bright young men to work 'with' him, not 'for' him."

"Sure, let me see it."

I reached over to get the card, but before I could get to it, Sue began to read.

"It says 'Eric J. Metzger, Representative of Kaysam, Manufacturer of Waterproof Boots'. Eric's address is in Englewood Cliffs, New Jersey. That's right over the George Washington bridge. It's an easy ride from here. I'll bet you could make a pretty penny selling boots."

Sue was nodding affirmatively.

Sue pleaded, "Let me introduce you to one of these business persons. They'll do anything for me as long as they think I'll sleep with them. Then instead of you moving to the West Side, come live with me until you start making a decent salary again."

Sue returned my gaze.

"Wow! What a magnificent offer. But I can't. I won't put you in that kind of position. I love you for saying all that you are saying, but my mind is made up."

I leaned over and kissed Sue's cheek. It was soft and cool.

Sue whimpered, "I guess I should give up. You are hell-bent on destroying yourself. I think all I can do is make love with you tonight. I know that when you move, we won't see much of each other. In fact, will we see each other at all? But I'm going to try to make sure you'll never want to leave the East Side after I get through with you tonight."

How lucky could I be? I smiled. "Keep on bragging. I'm all yours."

27

CHARLIE IS LOOKING FOR THE MISSING BOTTLE OF VODKA

I stayed the night with Sue. I kissed her lips as she lay sleeping. The next morning, I skipped my way down the stairs to my apartment. I wanted to get an early start. I knew Arnie would get to Brandy's early. He did this to check and set up everything. Arnie was a diligent owner.

I showered and headed straight for Brandy's. When I arrived, Bobby Hebb, the singer, was rehearsing a new song. He said it was called *Sunny*. I thought it had potential. At least I hoped it did.

I greeted both Bobby and Arnie, "Hi! How's it going?"

"Hey." Bobby winked at me. "Why are you wasting your time at Lloyd's? You gotta see the chicks we have coming in here. One after another."

Bobby grinned.

"He's right on," Arnie confirmed.

Arnie placed an empty wine glass down on the bar.

"We don't have any complaints regarding your sandwiches. They are selling quite well and pleasing a lot of customers."

Arnie smiled.

"But we heard you are moving to the West Side. Is that true?"

Arnie looked puzzled. Before I could answer, Arnie looked worried.

"Will that affect your business with us?"

I stated, trying to assure Arnie, "Of course not. Nothing will be even a tiny bit different."

Bobby Hebb yelled out, "You ought to see our waitresses! One of them is so hot she's going out with Bill Cosby the famous comedian."

Bobby strummed a note on his guitar.

I nodded. "Sounds like everything is running well, including the hot and cold babes you have coming in and out every night."

Bobby Hebb smirked. "You gotta know it."

"Okay. I'm off to Lloyd's. See you both soon."

When I arrived at Lloyd's, Charlie was wiping down the bar.

"Just the guy I wanted to see this morning. I heard you were moving next week."

I confirmed as I slid onto a bar stool, "It's the gospel."

Charlie continued to wipe the bar, "Well, here's the deal. There's this girl I've known for a long time. She recently dropped out of Skidmore. She's coming into the city tomorrow. She's looking for a place to live. I'd like to check out your place for her."

"Fine, when would you like to go there?"

"How is right now before it gets busy?" Charlie tossed the rag into a container.

"Sure, Let's go."

I headed out the door, followed by Charlie. We walked briskly to my apartment and took the elevator to the third floor.

"I'd like to look around."

Charlie opened the bathroom door. He pulled the shower curtain back as if something might pop out at him from inside. He looked at the bathtub as if it might contain a hidden treasure.

Charlie grunted, "I guess it's not there. I was sure I'd find the bottle of vodka hidden there."

I raised my voice, almost yelling, "I don't have your

bottle of vodka."

I was frazzled.

Charlie demanded, "Then where is it?"

Charlie changed the subject as he opened a cabinet in the kitchen.

"Anyway, she's going to be here tomorrow. I'd like you to show her your apartment when she gets here."

Charlie continued looking everywhere in my studio 'no bedroom' suite. Eventually he stopped.

"I don't see it. Let's go back to the bar."

Charlie headed out my apartment door. We walked hurriedly back to Lloyd's.

On the way, Charlie rubbed my shoulder, then squeezed it, "Yeah, maybe it will be good day for us both."

"Hope so."

I couldn't believe what I just witnessed! *This fucker really thinks I stole his lousy bottle of vodka. He thinks, or at least thought, that I might hide it in my bathtub. Of all places, that would be the last place someone would hide anything. Never mind a bottle of vodka.*

"By the way, Meg will be at your place tomorrow at about 11'ish. Her full name is Meg Colter. She'll ring your bell for you to buzz her in."

Charlie was tightening his grip on my shoulder as we approached Lloyd's.

"Okay, I'll be glad to give her a scenic tour of my one room apartment, including the kitchen and my luxurious toilet."

I pulled away from Charlie as I opened the door and walked into Lloyd's.

Charlie and I didn't exchange another word that entire day and night.

***

The bell went off at about 10:50 the next morning. She called up on the speaker in the lobby.

"It's Meg Colter. I'm here to check out your apartment. I'm a friend of Charlie's."

I called down, "I'll buzz you up. I'm in 310. C'mon up. I'll leave the door ajar. See you in two minutes."

She smiled as she entered my place. *Wow! What a beauty!* Short brown hair, gorgeous hazel eyes. She was wearing tight-fitting jeans, which showed off her beautiful legs. Her loosely fitting white blouse left little to my imagination. Her eyes were darting everywhere, although there wasn't much to see.

"Looks nice. Pretty much what I'm looking for. How much is the rent here?"

"I can tell you what I'm paying, but the landlord may have a different price for you. My lease is up. Who knows?"

I opened the bathroom door for Meg to peek in.
Meg snickered, "Only one toilet seat."
She checked herself out in the mirror.
I laughed. "That's usually how they come."
Meg pondered a moment. "Why are you leaving?

This is such a nice cozy place. Charlie tells me you are the cook, so to speak, at Lloyd's. I know Lloyd's is right down the street. It's an easy walk. What's up? Why would you leave this place?"

Meg looked puzzled.

"I just quit my day job. Right now, I can't make enough money to cover the rent. I'm paying $145 per month here. I just signed a lease for an apartment on the West Side for $85 per month."

Meg walked over to the kitchen.

"That's quite a difference in rent. I can understand why you'd leave. I like the place. It's just what I'm looking for if the rent is close to what you are paying."

Meg looked at the stove and opened the oven door.

"Does everything work?"

I opened the refrigerator and freezer doors.

"Everything works beautifully. Put your hand in here and feel how frozen that bag of peas is. Believe me, I've cooked a lot of meals here. I've made a lot of people happy right in this very place. And since you wanted to know why I'm leaving here, I'll ask you the same question. Why are you leaving Skidmore? Is it true you were in your junior year there?"

I closed the doors. Meg came out of the kitchen and walked over to the window.

She commented sarcastically, "Nice view. I guess if you like looking down at 85th Street, you can't beat it."

Meg paused, then continued, "Skidmore . . . bad fit!

I've no idea what the hell I was thinking three years ago. All girls! All fucking girls! I like boys. I like the way boys talk. I'm not one of those girls that gets all prissy when guys go gross. I enjoy it. The grosser the better. In fact, it can turn me on."

Meg turned away from the window and looked back at me. She pointed to the mattress.

"I'm sure you are taking it."

Meg walked over to the mattress and sat down at the end.

"Comfy."

She sighed. I returned Meg's gaze. I wasn't sure what to say or do. *Was she a girlfriend of Charlie's? What was* their relationship?

"I'll be glad to give you the landlord's phone number."

I picked up my notebook and tore out a page. I wrote down the landlord's number and handed Meg the paper. "Yes, I'm keeping the mattress."

Meg took the torn out page and placed it neatly in her pocketbook.

"I told Charlie I'd meet him at Lloyd's. I didn't tell him exactly when, since I didn't know how long I'd be looking at your place. But I'd be okay with walking over there now. How about you Robert? Do you want to walk over with me?"

Meg tightened her belt and slipped into the bathroom.

Meg left the bathroom door open.

I replied, "Thanks, but no. I'll be right along. Maybe a few minutes after you."

I could see she was brushing her hair and spraying something she had taken out of her purse. As Meg walked to the door to leave, she turned.

"See you at Lloyd's in a few minutes. I guess you should know, I'm going to ask Charlie if I can waitress for a few nights."

Meg left. All I could think was how upset Natasha would be. Natasha wasn't happy with seven nights. She wanted eight nights, like the Beatles had.

When I got to Lloyd's, Meg was talking to Charlie behind the bar. She waved at me as I headed to the kitchen to set up for the day and evening. A few minutes later Charlie strode in.

"How did it go with Meg?"

"We did fine. I think she'll rent the place."

Charlie smiled his gap-toothed smile as he told me, "You didn't make a move on her. She asked if you are a queer. The two of you were all alone and you did nothing but talk. It was one of the first times in her life she didn't feel sexy. Meg actually stated that as much as she hated Skidmore, she had a better chance of getting laid there than with you."

I didn't answer Charlie right away. I could only flash back to all my fruitless dates back in Boston. *It must be me. I'm the loser. Sue And Pat didn't count. They made it easy for me. They made the first moves. Pat stayed over the first night. She picked up her belongings the next day and parked them in my place. It had been Sue's idea to stomp. I'm the creep. How many women had I disappointed?*

I sighed and nodded to Charlie. "I'm sorry if I made Meg feel bad."

I went back into the kitchen. Natasha was waiting there for me. She was fuming.

"That prick Charlie is bringing in a new waitress. He wants her to have two of my nights. Did you know he was going to do that?"

Natasha fumbled with her apron.

"Not really, but I did meet her. Her name is Meg. I think she'll be moving into my apartment when I leave next Sunday. I guess Charlie has known her for a long time."

"That's going to really screw me up moneywise."

"Hey, I think you are overly concerned. Do you know how many bars and restaurants there are in this city? How about Elaine's? You could rub elbows with Bruce Jay Friedman. He's a very funny writer. It is hard to be funny in print. Maybe he is even funnier in person?"

Natasha looked a little less concerned.

"Maybe, you could help me at Brandy's?"

"I'll talk to Arnie, but I'd try places that serve more expensive food. I just heard about a steak place in the

Village called O'Henry's that is jammed."

I was having a hard time hearing and talking above the jukebox. Someone had raised the volume. It was blaring out *On the Wings of a Dove*. I tried to console Natasha, raising my voice to be sure she heard me.

"There is always waitress turnover. You'll be fine, despite that prick Charlie."

***

The rest of the week was passing quickly. Ira came by and he brought a friend. Natasha sat them down at The Table. I walked towards The Table. Ira was smiling and pushing himself up. He had one hand out towards me, the other on his friend's shoulder.

"Hey there, Robert, I want you to meet my buddy Jules Garfunkel. He's Artie's brother. Remember I told you I grew up on the same street as the Garfunkels."

At the same time Jules extended his hand out to me.

"Great to meet you, Mr. 'Fairly Famous.'"

I grinned and shook Jules's hand.

"Did you guys play *The Sound of Silence*?"

They both nodded at once.

Jules began to speak, "Yeah, we plead guilty. We both agreed this place needed some really good music and some fabulous lyrics. For twenty-five cents we did this place a big favor."

I looked over at the jukebox.

"I love that song too. I actually really like everything

your brother and Paul Simon write and sing. I'm also impressed that they used their real Jewish names."

Jules touched his chin.

"Yeah, when they first started out, they called themselves, 'Tom and Jerry.' I don't know how the jukebox guy found *The Sound of Silence*. As far as I know it's only been part of an album called *Wednesday Morning, 3 A.M*. I heard from Artie that Paul wrote a song called *He Was My Brother*. It was also on the *Wednesday Morning, 3 A.M.* album."

"I never heard that song. What brother? Whose brother?"

Jules looked sad. He was actually shaking.

"Artie had written it as a general sort of statement, but then when everything went so wrong, he dedicated it to Andrew Goodman. Andrew was friends with both Artie and Paul. He was one of the guys killed down in Mississippi. He was down there helping to register Negroes to vote. The Ku Klux Klan murdered three of them . . . Chaney, Goodman, and Schwerner."

I grimaced. "Awful story. I remember reading about it. One columnist wrote that if all three boys had been black, no one would have heard a word about it."

Ira was almost crying as he agreed, "Probably true and you know *The Sound of Silence* in its own way symbolizes that incident and this country."

I got up and dropped my quarter in the jukebox. The song began again. I looked at Ira.

"*The Sound of Silence* is one of the most played songs here, but I don't think that anybody here thinks in those terms. I doubt that they even hear the lyrics."

Jules smiled up at me as I went to sit down.

"You probably just made my brother a little richer. I can't think of a more meaningful way to do it."

I slapped the table.

"That song resonates with me. I'm jealous of someone who not only writes brilliantly, but is able to put the lyrics to beautiful music. What a wonderful gift to have been able to give to a friend, especially when there is little else you could do."

"Yup, I know what you mean. I'm not sure who does what with their music. I don't ask Artie. But we all have to agree that Artie has an awesome voice. His voice makes their tribute to Andrew that much more poignant."

Jules looked sadly over at the jukebox that was playing his brother's record. Ira had been listening to every word.

"I think it's all been said. I knew Andrew. I was with Abbie the day the news broke. I'll never forget the look on Abbie's face. Look around the bar or anywhere for that matter. You'll see and hear the 'Sound of Silence.' It's called apathy."

Jules nodded in agreement.

"Abbie deserves a ton of credit for going back down there."

Ira moved closer to the table.

"Yes, he does. But I'm going to change the subject to something much lighter before we all end up crying our eyes out. I wanted to mention that I picked up a used surfboard for all of us to use at Jones Beach. Maybe we can get there as early as late June."

"What a great 'change of subject'! I've always wanted to try surfing. I skied a lot back home. Maybe there is a connection?"

Ira caught my eye.

"Of course there is. It's called balance. Well, summer is a way off. We came here to munch on one of your sandwiches. Would you be kind enough to slice up two thick and juicy ones along with two sides of potato salad?" "Coming right up. Many thanks for dropping by. The sandwiches are on me, but please leave Natasha a nice tip or I'll have hell to pay."

I put my hand out again towards Jules.

"I can't wait to go to the beach with you both. Hey, Jules, hope you won't mind if I play some Dylan tapes on the way to the beach."

Jules grinned back.

"I like a lot of the young singers besides my brother, Bob Dylan included."

"Hope you'll come back soon. It's pretty much me and my roast beef sandwiches here at Lloyd's."

I headed back to the kitchen.

I heard Ira call out taunting me, "I suppose we

should feel sorry for you, especially when we look around this place and see so many luscious lovelies that may be available to you. Remember, Abbie told you that women love to be fed. Believe me, Abbie knows a lot about women!"

I looked back at Ira and Jules.

"You are right. I can't complain. Can I?"

The jukebox kept playing song after song. It seemed that Ira and Jules had probably got everybody started. All of a sudden, the jukebox was jumping. Somebody played *Little Sister* by Elvis three times. Someone else played *Let's Twist Again, Like We did Last Summer*. Whoever was playing it, played it more times than I could count. It did get people moving even while they were at the bar sitting on a stool. Their bodies were gyrating and their hands were clapping somewhat in time with the music. I was just hoping they didn't fall off their stools. Somebody standing in front of the juke played, *Runaround Sue* by Dion. He turned towards the bar and pointed to a very attractive girl sitting on one of the stools.

He yelled out, "Her name is Sue!"

I'd have to ask my Sue what she thought of the song. Minutes later Dick came in with a huge smile. He walked over to the jukebox and played *Running Scared* by Roy Orbison. Once again, I was on my way back to the kitchen.

"What's up?" Dick asked as he walked from the

jukebox over to me.

I stopped to really look at Dick. "What's up with you? How come you have that bigger than ever grin on your face? What did you swallow? And if you are so happy why did you play *Running Scared*?

Dick suddenly looked serious. "I just asked Beverly to marry me. You know what's so scary is she said 'Yes.'"

I pumped Dick on the back. "Congrats, old man. What are you drinking?"

"Thanks. I think I need a bunch of napkins, more than I need a drink."

Dick reached behind the bar and grabbed a few napkins.

"I can barely support myself. I'm worried. How will I be able to support two people?"

Now Dick was vigorously wiping both his hands.

"I don't blame you for worrying, but with your personality and your smile you'll be fine."

I put both my thumbs up.

Dick looked back at me. "I really appreciate your confidence. The other good thing is Bev is laid back. I don't mean that sexually. Bev's a good sport and that's why I fell for her."

Dick continued to dry his hands. I couldn't help laughing.

"Funny, I just had a crazy cab ride to the courthouse downtown with Sue. But that's another story. What was so nutty was the cabbie. He thought Sue and I were going there to get married."

Dick stopped wiping and looked up at me.

"I guess anybody might think that."

"He spent the entire ride telling me all the things wrong with marriage. At least his marriage! Sue tried to get him to shut up by saying that neither of us popped the question. It didn't work. He rambled on and on."

Dick scratched his head.

"Well, what were you going to the courthouse for if not a marriage license?"

"I'll tell you the whole story later this week when Bev joins us. Maybe Sue can make it too. We'll celebrate your proposal and Beverly's 'yes.' In our case, we will celebrate getting out of that cab alive. While he was telling me why not to get married, he kept turning his head to look at me. Not a cool idea when driving in this city."

I turned my head, imitating the cabbie. Dick smiled.

"I know what you are saying. Okay let's try to find a night next week the four of us can get together."

"It will have to be a night that will work for Sue. I'll check when Sue can make it. You check with Beverly."

I walked back to the kitchen.

28

I FINALLY MOVE

Once again Sunday morning showed up like it usually does, right on time. Jake was ringing my bell at 7:30. I buzzed him up.

"Well," Jake smirked as he looked around and asked skeptically, "are you ready to move? You know I'm due at Lloyd's a little before noon. Let's get this show on the road, Hopalong. Did you get your old rattletrap of a car out of the stable?"

"Yeah, I got it out last night. It cost a fortune, but cheaper than parking tickets."

Jake motioned for me to hurry with his hands. I groaned. Jake didn't appear to be listening as he looked around.

"You haven't got much here to move, thank

goodness."

We carried the stuff down. It only took two trips. We stuffed it all into my banged up red Chevy II that had survived the Bronx. We drove off to West 88th Street. Jake and I didn't say much until we arrived when Jake said, "Did you realize that Diane Bishop lives two buildings from your place?"

Jake pointed his finger at her building.

I replied, "Diane handed me a note at the Simon and Garfunkel concert. It had her phone number and address on it. I hadn't really looked at it until I found it in my pants as I was getting my stuff ready and I said to myself . . . wow . . ."

There wasn't a lot of stuff to carry up. The biggest problem we had was the mattress. Somehow we managed, with me at the top and Jake pushing from the bottom, to get it up four flights to its new home. The few chairs and all the rest of my limited stuff, we took up pretty quickly.

We sat down in what would be my living room. We both needed to catch our breath. I offered Jake a cup of tea. Jake put his hands up indicating "no" to tea now. Jake had very expressive hands. I asked Jake when he wanted to leave for Lloyd's.

"Soon. Are you going to call Diane?"

"Sure. I've been thinking about it. What's with you and Diane?"

I put the cup back in the sink. Jake seemed annoyed

as he looked around my not too spacious apartment.

Then Jake declared, "When we were at the Garfunkel concert either Diane or I explained that we are just bagel buddies at our workplace. She's a piece of work. She is all of that and then some. She's very smart. She's also very volatile. Diane has a boyfriend named Murray who lives down in the village. He's always telling her she has 'shit for brains.'

"Before Murray, she had a boyfriend who was totally devoted to her. He's a buddy of mine. His name is Ivan. He'd still do anything to get her back. Ivan happens to be a really nice guy."

I mused, "Sounds like Murray and Diane have a very unhealthy relationship. Why do you think she goes for him?"

Jake began to explain, "Evidently, he gives her some great sex because, as she tells it, she goes to his place a lot."

Jake got up to look in the bedroom where we had just placed the mattress. Jake gave his somewhat snotty appraisal.

"Your bedroom is small, but larger than I would have expected."

Jake continued, "Who knows? Maybe she wants to find out if she really does have 'shit for brains.'

"You are the 'incredibly fucked up' expert. How fucked up is Diane?"

I got up to look in the bedroom to check on Jake's

comment. The bedroom had been one of the main reasons I had chosen this place. I did not have a bedroom on 85th.

Jake sneered, "Well, for Christ's sakes, I just told you that she is getting fucked regularly by some character in the Village who tells her she has 'shit for brains.' What would you say? Is she fucked up or not?"

I grinned. "I don't know. I have a strong feeling I'll find out for myself. Anyway, I'll go over to Lloyd's with you whenever you are ready."

I went back to the living room where we had placed a few chairs. Jake eased himself into one of the chairs. He had his hand on his lower back.

He was quietly moaning, but stopped to ask, "What's with you and Sue?"

I looked back at Jake.

"It can't be the same. It will never be as convenient as it was for both of us, but we are still very much in like. Sue is very special. I'm sure we'll work something out."

We headed back to Lloyd's. It was getting close to noon. We made it there very quickly, even though we were coming from the West Side. I began to slowly walk with Jake toward the kitchen. I glanced over at The Table and was very surprised to see Natasha just about to sit down. She motioned at me to come over. She had a beautiful smile, showing off two beautiful dimples. I had never noticed that she had dimples. The jukebox was blaring out *Stand by Me* by Ben E. King.

Natasha continued to smile broadly, as she made it clear that I should sit down.

"I got here only a few minutes before you did. Boy, did you steer me right. I was at Elaine's this morning. I was able to meet Elaine and we were the perfect fit. She needed a waitress for Sunday and Monday evenings. Guess what? I start next Sunday. By the way, I loved her humongous glasses. I never saw glasses that large before."

"Great!" I enthused. "Did you get a chance to look at their menu? They have some interesting prices."

Natasha began to chuckle. "Of course I did. Could be some fat tips. Elaine also showed me around. From across the room, she pointed out the writers' tables. She whispered that there are very special people who sit at those tables."

I was somewhat annoyed. "Like how? What makes them so special?"

Natasha nodded knowingly. "They are all writers. Many are famous. Some, according to Elaine, will become famous. Elaine explained that the average Joe or Jane will come there to check out the writers. Sometimes they'll even ask them for autographs."

Natasha made a funny disgruntled face.

"That's the face Elaine made when she whispered that some ask for autographs."

Natasha then pointed at Meg who was taking sandwich orders from a table of guys. Meg was laughing quite loudly.

Natasha noted, "I can see you are well covered here on Sundays. Have you met her yet?"

I looked over at Meg, "Yes."

"She's very pretty, but 'ho-hum' pretty. Anyway, let me tell you more about Elaine's and some of the writers."

Natasha was breathing heavily.

"Okay, but tell me first. What is 'ho-hum' pretty?"

"Oh, she's pretty, but not nearly as pretty as she thinks she is. I'm a Russian maidel. I know these things."

Natasha smiled again.

"More importantly, let me tell you about Elaine's."

I looked back at Natasha. "I have never seen you this happy."

"Okay, okay, are you going to let me talk? Then Elaine ushered me over to the so-called writers' tables. She introduced me to them all. 'This is Natasha. She will be waiting on you all on Sundays and Mondays. I want you all to behave and keep your hands in your pockets.'

"Elaine then in a hushed voice did a *Who's Who*. 'The tall guy dressed in all white is Tom Wolfe. You'll notice he loves talking with Jimmy Breslin about New York. He's working on something that I think he calls *Radical Chic*. I believe it might have to do with Leonard Bernstein, the famous composer. But don't quote me. I just get to hear tidbits.'

"Elaine gently pushed me a little closer to the writers and went on, 'I love it when Jimmy and Tom talk. They are the odd couple. Jimmy is more or less rumpled when dressed and Tom is meticulously dressed. I often wonder how Tom doesn't get any of those white suits stained, especially given all my sauces. Jimmy almost always seems to bring up Branch Rickey's name whenever the guys are talking sports.'

"She then pointed out someone named Pete Hamill and the chap you mentioned, Bruce Jay Freidman. She spoke softly, 'Bruce is a funny guy. He's working on a lot of comedic books. I hear maybe a movie or two. Pete is a columnist for The Herald Tribune. I might say one of the best.'"

Natasha was bubbling over. "Robert, I have to tell you, I was so impressed. This was early yet. I suspect more celebrity types will be coming into Elaine's perhaps a little later. I believe this Russian maidel is going to be just fine."

I smiled at Natasha. "I'm in your corner. You are a fighter. I love that about you."

Natasha shook her head.

"I'm trying. Oh, there's more. After I left Elaine's I went over to Malachy's Bar and Grille. I actually got to talk to Malachy for a few minutes. At least I thought the owner was Malachy, but he informed me that both his brother and father were named Malachy. He introduced himself as Frank McCourt. At this time, he didn't need any more waitresses, but he took down my name and phone number."

"Great! You are on a roll."

I touched the back of Natasha's hand.

Natasha had more to say. "Mr. McCourt asked me if I had checked any other restaurants. I told him Elaine's. I mentioned being shown the writers' tables and some of the writers. Mr. McCourt laughed. He wanted me to know that he was writing a book as well. He couldn't wait for that smart-ass group over there to read his book. He was going to call it *Angela's Ashes*. He was very nice to me and wished me good luck."

I took my hand from Natasha's hand and put both my thumbs up.

"Wow! You really got around."

Natasha suddenly looked at me with concern.

"The other night when you left a little early, Charlie was telling everybody at the bar about Meg starting Sunday. He yelled out, 'Wait until you see Meg. Robert had his chance with her. He blew it!' Charlie was laughing. Then Charlie added that Meg took your apartment. He's pretty sure she's paying a lot less than you did. Evidently the landlord took a liking to her."

I'd heard enough.

I told Natasha, "Goodbye, until I see you Tuesday. Appreciate all the info."

29

A WALK IN THE PARK

AS I HEADED back to my new apartment, I thought I'd call Diane. I'll bet she can clue me in about the West Side. After all she probably spent four years at Barnard, which is on the upper West Side and now she's here on West 88th Street. She can tell me where to go. She can tell me what's happening around here. She can show me the ropes. I found the slip of paper Diane had given me. I unrumpled it and called her.

"Is this Diane Bishop?"

"This is she. With whom am I speaking?"

Diane sounded apprehensive.

"Do you remember me? I'm Robert. We met at the Simon and Garfunkel concert."

"Yes."

Diane now sounded pleased. "You were sitting next to me. You came with someone named Sue."

"Right! Are you ready for this? You'd better sit down." "I'm already sitting. What's the big news? What should I get ready for?"

"Well, I just moved from the East Side to right next to you on West 88th Street. I myself was surprised. I was pleased when I looked at the address you handed me at the concert."

"Well, why were you pleased? I thought you had a girlfriend. I assumed it was Sue. I also thought you were busy making a lot of people deliriously happy with your roast beef sandwiches. By the way, I've never gotten even one."

I laughed. "Boy you are assertive! I called because I'm totally unfamiliar with the West Side. I thought you might show me around. I also was told you have a boyfriend."

Diane laughed back. "You must have been speaking with Jake. Yes, I have one. At least I think I do most of the time. He lives down in the Village. I'm sure Jake already clued you in. Anyway, just in case you don't know everything about me, his name is Murray."

"Would you like to go over to Broadway and have a bite to eat? Or maybe just coffee?"

Diane seemed to pause for a moment and then breathed into the phone, "It's Sunday. My favorite thing to do on Sunday is walk over to Central Park. I'd love to just have a stroll. This way I'll get a chance to bore the hell out of you by telling you all about myself and then when I'm finished you can do the same. Just kidding."

"What time will you be ready?"

"I'll be down in a flash. I'll meet you in front of my building in seven minutes."

"Great!"

I checked my watch. I tore down my steps and waited in front of her building. There were a few people hanging out between her building and mine. The smell of marijuana wafted through the air. I nodded to the smokers. They didn't nod back. I kept looking at my watch. It was exactly seven minutes when Diane came bursting through her building's door.

Diane was quite attractive. One might call her petite. She had very blonde hair, blue eyes, and very fair skin. My eyes were very pleased.

Diane smiled. "You look the same as you did a month ago."

"I would hope so. Is that a good thing or a bad thing?"

Diane was laughing. "A neither thing. Let's see how our walk goes."

I strode beside Diane.

"How come you gave me your address at the concert?"

"I'm not sure I remember why. Jake had mentioned

you more than once. Jake likes you, although he says you have a sharp tongue. I'm not sure what that means."

I tapped Diane on the shoulder. "Jake has his own language. I'm sure you've noticed."

"He does. Maybe I liked the fact you were from Boston. I haven't met many of us Bostonians since I got here."

I was surprised. "I thought Barnard would have a lot of Bostonians."

Diane stepped up her stride as we approached Central Park.

"Probably. I guess I didn't get to meet many of them. I did meet one my freshman year. She was my mentor. G-D we hated each other. She was from Dorchester. That's where you are from. Right?"

I picked up my stride as well.

"Right, I am from Dorchester. What was her name?"

Diane made a face. "Lorraine Gold. I'll never forget that name."

I looked at Diane with disbelief. "You've got to be joking. She's my sister-in-law."

Diane looked frazzled. "I'm very sorry. I'm sorry that she's your sister-in-law. I'm sorry that I said what I said."

"You only said that you both hated each other. Sounds like a fair fight to me."

Diane grabbed my hand to cross Central Park West. "C'mon, let's hurry before the cars come at us. You know in this town they don't stop."

Diane and I rushed across. As we entered the park, the air was fresher and the rumble of the traffic was muffled.

Diane breathed deeply.

"We made it one more time! I've only been here once. Jake got a group of guys here to play softball."

"I don't play softball. But I'm a movie person. I love the movies. Do you know that Bette Davis is also from Lowell?"

I began to look around. "I also like movies. Did you see *From Here to Eternity*? I loved the beach scene with Burt Lancaster and Deborah Kerr."

Diane shook her head. "Yes, I saw it. It was okay. But what I've been viewing are foreign movies. There are two theatres on Broadway that play foreign movies quite a lot. One is the Thalia, and the other is the New Yorker. I go to both of them all the time."

I was disappointed that Diane didn't share my fascination with the beach scene—their bodies, the rolling waves, the way they gazed at each other—but I kept pace with Diane, who was a fast walker.

"I don't know much about foreign films. I know they all have subtitles."

Diane slowed down and looked at me quizzically. "My boyfriend Murray and I go to these theatres every chance we get. He's divorced and has a young child. He's not available as much as I'd like. We just saw *Jules and Jim* Friday night."

I looked back at Diane. "Did you like it?"

Diane came to a complete stop and looked at me with disbelief.

"Are you kidding? We loved it. We read the reviews after we got back to his place. Murray won't read a review until after he sees the movie. He doesn't want to be influenced one way or the other."

"Sounds like a terrific evening," I ventured.

"Terrific isn't enough to describe it. The sex that night was as good as it gets. I get off on movies. They get me so horny, I think I'm going to explode."

Diane began to walk again, but more slowly as she asked, "Who are the reviewers you follow?"

As I was trying to think of an answer, Diane looked back at me again.

"I'm going to have to movie 'wise' you. I think you'll make a good pupil. One reviewer writes for *The Village Voice*. His name is Andrew Sarris. Another writes for *The New Yorker Magazine*. Her name is Pauline Kael. These are the most important movie voices. It's also important to make note of the directors. They have more to do with the success of a movie than the actors."

Diane looked at me knowingly. I kept up with her pace that seemed to be changing according to what she was saying.

I asserted, "I went to the movies without thinking about all that. I just went and either enjoyed or not. I never thought of movies being such a big deal."

Diane came to a stop and looked at me.

"Well I do. Movies are very important to me. I thought I made that very clear. I told you what happened after seeing *Jules and Jim*."

I stared back at Diane. "What's playing at those theaters tonight? I'm crazy about horny women."

Diane smiled.

"The next movie I want to see is *Knife in the Water*. It was directed by a young Polish director named Roman Polanski. Some say he will be considered one of the very best very soon."

I reached out and touched Diane's shoulder.

"When is it playing? Which theatre will be showing it?"

Diane stopped walking. "Let's head back. It will be at the Thalia next Sunday evening. Usually most movies start there at 7:00. Do you think you can join me?"

I stopped beside Diane. "Sounds great. I'm very sure I can make it."

Diane looked pleased.

"After the movie there is a great place to get a hamburger on Broadway. Speaking of food, I go to 'Barney Greengrass, the Sturgeon King' every Sunday morning. If I call you, will you join me for breakfast next Sunday morning?"

I smiled happily. "Love to. I'll have to check with Jake. He covers for me most every Sunday. But even if he can't cover for me later in the day, I'm sure I can meet you at Barney's. What time do you usually get there?"

Diane was fumbling for her house key.

"Usually about 8:30 before it gets too crowded."

I leaned over and kissed Diane on the cheek. "Thanks very much for the 'stroll.' I enjoyed the conversation a lot. I hope you did as well."

"Of course, I did. I did most of the talking. I don't get to do that much speaking when I'm with Murray. He dominates."

Diane held her key up. "I found it. Do you and Sue talk much?"

I touched Diane's hand. "I think so, but Sue wants to know more about me. She says I'm very secretive."

Diane began moving towards her front door. "It sounds like we have a lot to talk about. Sue sounds interesting. I liked her very much the night of the concert, although we didn't get much time together."

"I believe I'll have to kiss your other cheek. It looked jealous to me. Then I'll take my leave. I'm going over to Lloyd's. Jake is there most Sundays. I need to see him."

I leaned over and kissed the other cheek.

Diane touched her finger where I kissed her. "That felt just right. Say hello to Jake for me, although I'll see him tomorrow at work. Jake will have tea. I'll have coffee and most likely a bagel or two."

"I'm off."

I waved goodbye to Diane and she turned and put her key in the lock.

30

THE BOTTLE OF

VODKA IS FOUND

I MADE IT over to Lloyd's fairly quickly. I walked by the bar and headed to the kitchen. The Jukebox was playing, *Will You Love Me Tomorrow?* by the Shirelles.

Jake greeted me with a big sigh. "Very glad to see you. I could use your help today. I'm tired for no damn good reason."

"My pleasure. I will take over for you today, but I'd appreciate it if you cover for me one evening this week. I can be here till about six, but then I'd like to take Sue, Dick, and Beverly out for dinner. I want to congratulate

Dick and Bev. They are going to get married. I'll ask Sue what night will work for her. I'll let you know as soon as I know."

"Yeah, I'm free every night this coming week, except Saturday. I have a date Saturday night. It's my second date with this girl named Linda. I only met her a week ago. She seemed really special. I hope I don't find out that she's really fucked up. So far, so good."

Jake gestured a thumbs up.

"Have you sold any sandwiches today? "

Jake shrugged. "Yuh, it's been a good morning. We've already sold twenty-two sandwiches, plus fourteen salads. But I had to not only make everything, I had to bring all the food to the tables. That new waitress called in sick. I think her name is Meg. I've briefly met her," Jake said with a grunt.

"By the way, Arnie from Brandy's dropped by. He was looking for you. He also mentioned that Brandy's was doing well with the sandwiches."

"Thanks. Did he say anything about why he wanted to see me?"

Jake squinted as he dried his hands. "No, he didn't offer anything except to say hello. He did say when you got a moment to go over there."

"If you want you can take off, I'll handle it from here."

Jake smiled. "Thanks, Meg did say if she were feeling better, she'd get here."

"Before you leave, let's try to find that bottle of vodka. It should only take a couple of minutes."

Jake and I began pulling the clutter away from the slicer. There it was! Right where Charlie had put it when he told us "to guard it with our lives!" We looked at each other. We were frustrated that we had been so messy.

Jake pointed his finger at me. "You are the slob! It's not me. Anyway, Charlie will be pleased when he gets back. See you much later."

Jake shuffled off. The day stayed busy and Meg finally did show up. She arrived about five-thirty, a big relief since the place was beginning to get jammed. Some girl I hadn't seen before kept playing *Wooden Heart* by Joe Dowell. After she played that more times than I cared to count, she began to play *I've Told Every Little Star* by Linda Scott. I wasn't crazy about either song.

Meg came into the kitchen and greeted me like we had been best friends forever.

"Sorry I got here late. I had one of those mornings."

I didn't ask although my imagination pretty much guessed what "one of those mornings" was. I pointed at The Table and explained to Meg to try to keep it empty in case someone came in looking for me. Meg watched as I put a sandwich together.

"I really like the apartment. It feels just perfect. It's a short walk to Lloyd's. That's a bonus. Did you get to know anyone in the building? You lived there quite a while."

I thought there was no point in mentioning Sue or our arrangement.

"Yes, quite a few people. I'm sure you'll meet some soon."

Meg looked puzzled. "I did meet two guys. I believe their names are Paul and Chris. They were talking about having a party next Saturday night. I joined in, 'I'll be there if you invite me. What apartment will it be in?' I couldn't believe what happened next!"

Meg's eyes signaled disbelief. "They looked at each other and laughed. One of them seemed to think he was explaining when he stated, 'This is a party for swingers. Only men are welcome. You'd be the only girl. I don't think you'd be happy.'"

Meg touched my hand and looked at me questioningly.

"Yes, I knew them. They are nice guys. And yes, their names are Paul and Chris. They are a pair and they have a lot of similar friends. I had the same thing happen to me. They had a party about a month ago. They made it clear that I wouldn't be happy at their party."

Meg removed her hand. She seemed relieved.

"I'm glad you weren't welcome, Robert. I guess this town is swimming with them."

Meg looked at me for approval.

I whispered, "Hey, the fella who ordered the

sandwich will be pissed if you don't bring it to him quickly. Also, I see a few couples just came in. I hope they're hungry."

Time was flying by. It stayed busy throughout the evening. At about 8:45, Meg came back into the kitchen.

"There's someone sitting at The Table. He wants me to tell you that your friend Fred Joseph is here."

As I walked to The Table, the jukebox was playing *Hit the Road Jack* by Ray Charles. I remembered Fred loved that song. I looked out at The Table where Fred had a big grin on his face. He waved at me. I finished making two sandwiches, handed them to Meg, and went to greet Fred. Fred stood up as I got to The Table.

He grinned. "I have a brilliant idea. I'm heading to Boston tomorrow to meet one of my guys. I'll take two of your sandwiches with me. After I finish up with my meeting, I'll go over to Elsie's in Harvard Square and compare your sandwich to hers. You know damn well that she's the originator of the greatest roast beef sandwich ever made."

"What the hell will that prove? It's not a fair fight. My sandwiches will be a day old."

Fred grinned his special grin. "I'm going to eat one right now. I'll damn well remember how it tasted. Also, if your sandwich has any real character, one day shouldn't affect it one way or the other."

Fred pointed at Meg. "She's bringing me the two I

ordered. I can see she's already got one of them neatly wrapped."

I looked over at Meg as she brought the sandwiches to Fred.

I murmured, "Knowing you, you'll be rooting for Elsie's."

"Maybe so," Fred snickered. "Speaking of wrapping, have you wrapped up this waitress yet? I don't know how you can stand all these beautiful women around you every night. If you don't bag one a night, you are a loser. Maybe you are thinking of marrying Sue, you know the TWA flight attendant you introduced me to?"

"Whoa!" I exclaimed. "Why would you bring up marriage?"

Fred pointed at the ceiling. "Well, this place is wild. It's as if you had died and gone to heaven. You'd be crazy to even think of marriage. I'm off. I'll let you know how you made out in the contest."

31

MADGA, SUE, AND PALATSCHINKE

WHEN I GOT home that evening, I thought I'd give Sue a buzz. I needed to find out if or when she'd be available to meet Beverly and Dick for dinner.

"Hey there! What's going on with you?"

"Not much," Sue purred. "You sound far away. Where are you calling from?"

"I'm in my new digs on West 88th."

"Digs?" Sue laughed. "Since when do you use hip-slang talk? I am not sure I like it. But if you really want to know what's going on with me, then ask like you mean it."

I spoke very slowly, "Sorry, what's going on with you?"

"That's better. I miss you being right under me. I miss you a lot. How about you? Do you miss me?"

"Well, I'm calling. I called, believe it or not, to ask you out on a date."

"That will be a first." Sue laughed. "Where, when? What is it about?"

I explained, "I don't think you've met Beverly and Dick. I know them from Lloyd's. Dick has just proposed to Beverly. She said 'Yes.'"

"Are you telling me some good has come out of that stinking place?" Sue sighed. "I have Wednesday off. Does that work?"

"I know Dick always comes into Lloyd's on Monday after work. He has what he calls the Monday Blues. He works for his father. They don't get along well. I'm confirming that I'll pick you up. We'll walk over to one of Jake's favorite restaurants and meet them there."

Sue agreed, "Sounds like a plan. But what if they can't make it? Then we'll have to be alone with each other. I'm not sure that will work out."

Sue was giggling.

"I hadn't thought of that. Well, it would only be for a short while. I know I can handle it."

"I miss you," Sue exclaimed. "Who else can I have fun with like this? What time will you get here?"

"I'll be in your lobby at 6:30 p.m. That's this coming Wednesday."

I lowered my voice, "Can't wait to see you."

"Me too," Sue whispered. "It's ridiculous. It has been only a week or so, but it seems like ages since you moved." "I agree, I sooo miss the late evening stomps. Let's make up for lost time Wednesday evening."

Sue's voice was firm. "Better bring your toothbrush and dry underwear. I'm going to let you sleep over."

"I can't wait. I'm turned on already."

Sue laughed. "That's exactly what I like to hear. It's sweet music to my entire body. I hope you stay that excited for the next couple of days."

"Because you are a girl, you wouldn't know how painful it can be to be this excited. And not be able to clear the area or should I say 'ejaculate.' There's a name for the pain."

Sue tittered, "Yeah!"

Sue then raised her voice, "What's its name?"

I grimaced. "It's called 'Blue Balls.' I've had them before. Believe me, it's not tennis."

Sue was still laughing. "I'm very pleased to miss out on that little treat. But I can't say I'm sorry that you are THAT excited. See you Wednesday."

Sue hung up.

***

I was very pleased that Jake and I had found the bottle of vodka. I wasn't sure where Charlie was or when he would return. I couldn't wait to show it to him. I arrived at Lloyd's a little early. The place was pretty quiet. There was one couple sitting at a table. The jukebox was playing *So Much in Love* by the Tymes. I wondered if the couple had played it. They were holding hands and staring into each other's eyes. I figured they were good for maybe two months. This is New York and I had learned that things had a way of falling apart here.

Dick came in about six. He came directly to the kitchen to say hello. Dick looked very weary, but he still showed off his beautiful smile.

"What's going on?"

"The usual. I'd like to take you and Beverly to dinner Wednesday night. I want to congratulate you both. I'll bring Sue."

"Great!" Dick's smile grew even wider. "But we'll split the bill. I know you are really just getting started. You need every dollar. Also, I've got a real paying job, such as it is."

"I won't argue with you. It will be a lot of fun just to spend part of the evening out of Lloyd's."

Dick agreed.

"I'm looking forward to meeting Sue. I've caught glimpses of her. It will give you some time with Bev. You'll understand why even though I've got no right to get married, I did what I did. By the way, when is Charlie coming back?"

I took a look out at the tables to see if people were

arriving.

"As far as I know, Charlie will be back next week. I'm thinking Hungarian food. Jake found the place. He has a nose for great food and great prices. I've been there twice. Awesome restaurant!" I assured Dick.

"Of course Jake has a nose for great food. He works here most Sundays."

Dick looked at the roast beef on the slicer.

***

Wednesday evening I rang Sue's bell at 6:25. I looked through the glass on the inside door. There was Sue getting off the elevator. She smiled when she saw me.

"Let's go. I'm very hungry. Are they going to meet us at the restaurant?"

"Nope. Beverly evidently got called away. Dick asked if we could make it some other time. He was very apologetic."

Sue sighed and then began laughing. "Oh that's terrible. How are we going to get through the evening? Oh dear, just the two of us. What a shame. Where to?"

"My Budapest. It's on 78th and 2nd. I hope you like it as much as I do."

"I'm sure I will. I've been taken to a very fancy, expensive Hungarian restaurant by one of my passengers who wanted to get into my pants. The food was so good that I almost let him in. Why am I guessing this won't be as expensive?"

"You've always been a good guesser, but I think the

food is delicious. The service is special. Sort of like how your grandmother would want to wait on you if she could."

We picked up our pace. We were both very hungry.

I teased Sue along the way, "You are a pretty fast walker for someone your age."

Sue laughed and slapped me on my bottom.

"Look at who is talking about age. If I remember correctly, you will be twenty-four in one month. I'm only twenty-two. I told you that a long time ago."

As soon as we walked in, the owner came over to greet us.

"So wonderful to see you back. I like that you brought a new friend."

She looked at Sue. "You could do worse than Robert. I judge people by their appetite. Robert always orders the best dishes. Even when he comes with fuss bunny Jake!"

She touched Sue's wrist. "What's your name, my darling?"

Sue smiled at the owner. "It's Sue. Very nice to be here. I'm really looking forward to having dinner in your restaurant. Robert says everything is beyond best."

"I'll be your waitress tonight. I want to make everything extra special for you. I've never told my name to Robert or Jake, but now that I know you and your name, I'll tell you mine. My name is Magda."

Magda smiled at Sue. "I like the name Sue. I like

you even more than your name."

Magda then proceeded to usher us to a booth and commented with a wink, "This is the quietest booth in my restaurant and the most romantic!"

Magda went back to the kitchen and returned with two worn menus.

"Whenever you are ready, my dears, I'll be ready to take your orders."

Magda walked away, and then she suddenly turned to face me. She winked again. Magda then put both her thumbs up and smiled approvingly.

I looked over at Sue. Her face was beet red.

"I do believe Magda fell in love with you. Just like me with you, love at first sight."

I reached out to touch Sue's hand.

Sue opened the menu. "Let's first get down to basics. What should I order here? And then you can go on with your sweetie talk trying to bed me down."

I looked down at my menu. "I really don't need a menu here. The last three times I had the cherry soup first, then beef stroganoff, and palatschinke for dessert. I strongly recommend you do the same."

I squeezed Sue's hand.

"Okay." Sue nodded. "But what the hell is palatschinke?"

I laughed. "I'm sure you've had a Jewish blintz sometime, somewhere, in your life. If not, no matter. This palatschinke stands on its own two feet."

Magda was approaching our table with two wine glasses.

"I've got the perfect libation for two young lovers. It's a red wine. It's called *Egri Bikaver*—Bulls Blood. It will definitely mellow you both out. All your cares will be forgotten. You will be left with only love for each other. No charge. It's my gift to you both."

Sue smiled. "That is so nice of you. We both very much appreciate your warmth."

"I told Sue that not only is your food excellent, but your service is exquisite. This is beyond any of my expectations."

I caught Magda's eye. Magda laughed. "So what can I make for you two?"

I looked up at Magda. "You know very well what I get every time I've come here."

Magda nodded. "Cherry soup, beef stroganoff and palatschinke for two. Coming up, but not right up. I can see you two need some time to talk."

Sue watched as Magda walked back to the kitchen.

"What a find this place is. Magda is a treasure. I love it. I want to come here every night. Can we? Can we?"

I looked at the delighted, delightful Sue. "Not sure how you do it, but you really bring out the very best in people."

Sue tapped her fingers on our table. "So how come I have such a hard time bringing out the best in you? I can't get you out of the stinking bars. I don't know what more I can do for you. I gave you those business cards that I collected. I'm sure you haven't reached out to any of them."

"Not yet."

"Not yet! Why do I think 'not yet' might mean never? Anyway, let's talk about other stuff."

"Like what do you have in mind?"

"Okay, us."

Sue raised her wine glass. "Do you remember our first toast? I believe it was friends forever, or something close."

I raised my glass and we clinked. "I believe you are right. Let's say it again. Friends until we die. We are being that. How could it be any better?"

"How?" Sue shook her head in disbelief. "You are my very best friend. I only want the best for you. But there I go again. As usual not getting anywhere. Anyway, let's talk about marriage. Not for us, but just in general. What are your thoughts about marriage, just generally speaking?"

I looked back at Sue as I put down my wine glass. "You heard the taxi driver. I'd lose all my friends. I don't have that many to begin with. I believe he was talking about male friends, as in hanging out with the guys."

I chuckled. "He was sure we were going to the courthouse to get married."

"He wasn't alone with that opinion." Sue blinked.

"Every one of those people, including the magistrate, thought they knew what was good for us, especially what was good for me."

"Marriage?" There was a question in my voice. "It's serious stuff. Kids? Mostly they go hand in hand with marriage. Then there is the climbing divorce rate. I never told you this before, but I used to pray that my parents would get a divorce."

I took another sip of the wine.

"This Bulls Blood isn't kidding. All you have to do is sniff it. It warms my very cockles."

Sue was laughing. "First I never heard of palatschinke. Now I don't know much about cockles. Is it something I should be aware of when we make love later tonight? That is if you behave. But seriously, why did you want your parents to get a divorce?"

Magda was bringing us the bowls of cherry soup.

I spoke up quickly, before Magda arrived, "So I could get some F'ING sleep. My dad came home very late every night. He played cards Monday, Tuesday, and Wednesday. He'd go to their room about midnight and the screaming would start."

Magda placed the bowls neatly in front of us.

She spoke warmly to Sue, "I want so much for you to love my soup. So much so that you will hurry back."

Magda gave me an approving look and headed back to the kitchen.

Sue dipped her spoon in the soup. "Delicious! Yum!

Where has this been all my life?"

Sue looked up from the soup. "But your parents had seven kids? How do you explain that?"

I looked down at my soup. "I can't. Maybe they never heard of contraceptives. The pill is new. Who knows? But thank goodness you are so careful. I can also say thank goodness they had seven children. I was, as you know, number seven. I'd sure worry a lot if our child came out of that beautiful body of yours. Anyway, let's get back to important issues like soup. I'm so glad you like Magda's soup."

"Like it? I loved it!" Sue almost shouted. "It tasted like the best dessert I'd ever had. Look, Magda is coming with the beef stroganoff and something else along with it."

Sue whispered as she squeezed my hand, "By the way, I'm very glad your parents had seven children."

"How is everything so far? You look pleased. The stroganoff has arrived, along with a side of my very special red cabbage. And the wine? Is there any other wine like Bull's Blood?" Magda noted.

Sue looked up at Magda. "This is so very wonderful. It is beyond anything I could or would have expected. You care so much. Thank you for making me feel so comfortable. I cannot wait to taste the rest of your dishes."

Magda sighed. "I'm so very pleased to have met you. You are so beautiful, so lovely."

She turned and walked slowly over to the bar. We dove into the beef. It was delicious.

I tapped Sue's fingers. "I told you Jake knew food and the right places."

Sue interrupted her enjoyment. "The Hungarian restaurant one of those fellows took me to was good, but nothing like this."

When Sue finished her food, she looked back at me. "Let's get back to our previous conversation. What else do you have to say about marriage?"

"Not much. My parents couldn't even watch TV without squabbling. They would call each other 'damn fools,' whenever one of them commented on anything."

Sue wiped her fingers with her burgundy cloth napkin. "I don't know why, but this place makes me think of your Pat. You told me she cooked this kind of food. Was it as good? If it was even close to this, you should never have let her out of your sight."

I squinted at Sue. "I thought we decided a long time ago that we weren't going to discuss Pat. But yes, she was a very good cook, though not quite as good as Magda."

Sue looked puzzled. "I never really got the details of the break-up."

"I guess that's because I didn't give them to you. Pat said some really nasty things. She wanted out and didn't know how to do it nicely."

I looked over towards the kitchen. "Our dessert

should be here any minute. You know it's interesting you bring up marriage and Pat in the same conversation. In a way, Pat and I were married for three months. We did everything together. We got along beautifully. The sex was superb. It was all better than best, but imagine if we had married. How messy and expensive a divorce would have been!"

Sue reached over and touched my hand. "You know what? I'll bet one day Pat will apologize, especially, if everything for her was as good as it was for you. Look here comes Magda with our dessert."

Magda placed the two dessert dishes in front of us.

She looked at Sue. "If this doesn't bring you back here nothing will."

Magda then turned to me. "You, I'm not worried about. I know you'll be back and soon. You should both eat and enjoy every morsel."

Magda bowed her head as if she were having some sort of spiritual moment. She then walked back to the kitchen before either one of us could respond.

The palatschinke was as good as I remembered it. I watched Sue scrape her plate.

"Some night so far."

"I agree." Sue laughed. "By the way, I've got a few more business cards."

Sue reached down and pulled up her pocketbook. She handed me three more cards. Two of them were from the shoe business.

"It seems shoe people travel a lot. Just this week I probably met six or seven shoe people."

"My brother Lou travels quite a bit. Remember I told you about him. He came into Lloyd's and had quite the conversation with Charlie. Lou sells for a shoe company."

"Speaking of your brother . . . All your siblings are married, right? How are their marriages?"

I looked around the restaurant. It was pretty full for a Wednesday night. I turned my focus back on Sue.

"I really don't know what goes on behind closed doors. Maybe they're all in some sort of denial. Who knows? Not me. Let's finish our wine and go back to your place."

"You know, every once in a while, you come up with a good plan. Tonight, you are flawless. I can hardly wait to pull your clothes off."

Sue reached across the table and pulled at my shirt.

We made record time back to Sue's. We were tearing off our clothes as quickly as humanly possible.

Sue, out of nowhere, began, "Before I enjoy your delectable body and you do the same with mine, how would you define our relationship?"

"Before I answer that question, which by the way is a penis deflator, I just remembered I forgot to pay the check."

Sue groaned. "Oh, my goodness! What can we do now? You are almost naked."

Sue started giggling. "I'd love to see you walk over there just the way you are right now."

I scratched my head. "I don't know if it was the wine or you that caused me to forget to pay the check. In any case, I'll go there tomorrow. I'm very sure Magda will understand."

"Robert, I want to pay half. It was all so beautiful. Also, I'd love an answer to the penis deflator question, or is the flaccid penis the answer?"

I looked over at Sue and caressed her naked thigh.

"Sue, how can I describe what we have? To me it's perfect. We rarely disagree, except about Lloyd's. Why mess up a perfect relationship with a label?"

Sue laughed and put her hand on top of mine. "You are so sneaky. What a clever way of telling me nothing."

"I didn't pay the check because I so wanted to make love to you, or maybe too much Bulls Blood. Either way, we are wasting very precious time."

I leaned towards Sue and began kissing her neck.

I whispered, "Maybe we should squabble more like my parents did. They were married for over forty years."

Sue began hugging me, pulling me closer to her body. "Maybe, but I don't think I could handle seven kids."

***

We awakened the next morning, still holding each other very tightly. Sue blinked her eyes and began climbing out of her bed.

"It was a truly wonderful night. I've got a couple of overnights coming up. I really won't be free until the middle of next week."

She then slapped my butt. "Do you think you can stay out of trouble?"

Sue smiled.

I pulled the covers off the bed. "Trouble?"

I looked up at Sue. "I believe you mean other women. We have never asked that of each other."

Sue had a washcloth in her hand. "No, we haven't, and we shouldn't start now, but it's hard to beat what we had last night and so many other amazing evenings."

"I agree."

I grabbed her washcloth and snapped it at her wrist. "Let's make certain we have many more last nights. I'll shower and go back to my place. Please call me when you get back. I'll let you know what Magda has to say about our running out last night."

***

I got to Magda's restaurant about 3:00 p.m. I figured she'd start getting ready for dinner about then. I had asked Natasha to hold the fort at Lloyd's for about an hour. She knew how to do everything as well as I did.

Magda was at the bar when I got there.

I called out to her, "I'm looking for my check from last evening."

Magda spun around. "You two were so busy talking, you two lovebirds. I didn't have the heart to interrupt.

Anyway, I'm not charging you for Sue's dinner. It's my treat. I wanted to adopt her. I wanted to bring her home. That is without you, my dear. I liked her very much!"

Magda chortled. "Only fooling. But when are you going to ask her to marry you? If you don't ask her soon, some smart guy will. Also, if you are so stupid as not to marry her, don't ask me to serve you again. I don't like feeding stupid people."

"That is so generous of you not to charge me for Sue. I imagine you'll add marriage counseling to the bill. How much do I owe for my dinner?"

Magda handed me the bill. It was $8.65. I handed Magda a $10.00 bill.

"Please keep the change. You were at your best last night in every way."

Magda went over to the cash register and counted out the change.

"This is my treat. Don't think you can ever take that away from me."

I thanked her again, threw her a kiss, and scurried off to Lloyd's.

32

JAKE BRINGS A DATE

THURSDAY WAS QUIET. Natasha was spending more time hanging out in the kitchen than usual.

"I'm really enjoying working at Elaine's. If I ever get five minutes in this crazy life of mine, I'll start reading again. When I was younger, I used to read a lot. Those writers at Elaine's are a fascinating group."

I gave Natasha my most interested facial expression. "What did you hear that caught your attention? Also, we have to speak louder! The jukebox keeps playing *I Will Follow Him* by Little Peggy March. I think that guy Billy is playing it over and over. He's Tedd's roommate. Tedd is the fella who goes out with Esther Nan Bell. She's the one who comes in on weekends from Vassar. I dislike Billy and I hate the song.

Let's try to drown it out with our conversation."

Natasha spouted, "Yeah, I've noticed Esther Nan. You seem hung up on her and that guy Tedd. I did a little snooping around for you. She sometimes comes here on Saturdays. The guys think she's very cute. She also seems very nice and polite. I also think that Tedd is charismatic. I believe Esther Nan seems to think so too. Everybody watches Tedd, especially Billy. But when Esther Nan's around, Billy gets very jealous. He begins to drink too much and keeps getting nastier and nastier. I've heard from the other Neighborhood Playhouse folks that Billy won't let Tedd bring Esther Nan back to their apartment."

Natasha continued, "Anyway, as I was saying before we got off on Tedd and Billy, I had the pleasure of waiting on Jimmy Breslin and Pete Hamill's table. They were discussing the old Brooklyn Dodgers. They kept calling them 'The Bums.' I overheard Mr. Breslin say that he was going to write a book about Branch Rickey. He asserted Branch Rickey deserves a lot of credit. He doesn't get enough recognition for changing the world of sports and for that matter 'this whole damn country!'"

"That's impressive. I definitely agree with Jimmy Breslin about Branch Rickey."

Natasha had me intrigued, and she knew it.

She went on, "Pete Hamill kept mentioning Jackie Kennedy. It was as if he knew her."

The jukebox was now playing *Walk Like a Man* by

the Four Seasons.

I asked Natasha, "Have you heard when Charlie is returning?"

Natasha replied cautiously, "I believe I heard both Gloria and Charlie will be here next Wednesday. The word is they are working on some major changes. Evidently, they are barely breaking even. At least that's what I heard."

***

The next few days passed quietly. My food was doing well. I called Arnie at Brandy's and told him I'd drop by Sunday morning. Sandwich sales were good.

I called Diane Thursday evening. "Hope I didn't wake you."

"No, not at all. I've been up reading. Are we still on for Sunday and the movie?"

Diane sounded excited.

"Yes, I'll be in front of my building at 6:30 Sunday evening. That will give us plenty of time to get good seats. Right?"

Diane hesitated. "I'm not sure. It's a bit of a walk to the Thalia. I never know how crowded it's going to be. Let's make our departure time 6:15 to be on the safe side. Hope you won't mind being with me a little longer." Diane chuckled.

"Okay, 6:15 it is. Speaking of being with you for a long time, I thought we were going to meet at Barney Greengrass's Sunday morning. I was looking forward to finding out why Barney is 'The Sturgeon King.'"

"Can't make it this Sunday. Let's postpone it to maybe next Sunday morning. I promise to teach you all of the West Side ropes before it's over." Diane chuckled again.

"Before what's over? We haven't even gotten started. Besides, you have this 'shit for brains' boyfriend Murray."

Diane seemed hurt. "Sounds like Jake has been squealing again. Let's try our best to keep my Murray and your Sue out of our discussion. Let's just enjoy the movies."

"Okay. Sounds like a good idea. What are you reading, if I may ask?"

"Have you ever heard of Gloria Steinem?"

"I think so. Something about her being a Playboy Bunny."

"Yeah, she was employed by the New York Playboy Club. She wrote an article called 'A Bunny's Tale.' It's a tell-all piece. She confides how bunnies are so poorly treated at these clubs. It's pretty disgusting. There is also a photo of her in a bunny suit. She's very attractive. After I finish this piece, I intend to take on Betty Friedan's, 'The Feminine Mystique.' That will not be as easy a read as the 'Bunny's Tale.'"

"I hear what you are saying. Women seem to want to learn more about women. I don't think I want to learn more about men than I already know. Please save the

Gloria Steinem article for me. I've never set foot in a Playboy Club. It definitely sounds interesting when written from a real Bunny's perspective."

"Okay, will do. We can talk about it after you've read it. Although it's not a pleasant piece. I hate it when women are subjugated."

"Meanwhile, see you Sunday at 6:15. I'm looking forward to a real movie date."

***

Friday was another busy evening. I noticed that even Natasha seemed somewhat pleased. It didn't happen often.

I was looking forward to Sunday. I couldn't remember if I'd ever seen a foreign film. Maybe *Rashomon* could be considered a foreign film, although the word *Rashomon* had been made part of the American vocabulary. Anyway, Diane sounded like she knew a lot about movies. Especially foreign ones. I thought it could be very interesting in many ways.

Saturday was probably the busiest I had ever seen Lloyd's. The sandwiches were flying out of the kitchen. Natasha was constantly smiling. The jukebox was blaring out one song after another. *People* by Barbra Streisand was played the most. I laughed to myself remembering what Sue had to say about the *People* song.

A couple I hadn't seen before kept playing *Be My*

Baby by the Ronettes. They couldn't stop hugging each other.

A few minutes later, Natasha came into the kitchen.

She tapped me on the shoulder and pulled me out to see. "Give a kook. Do you believe it? It's Jake sitting at The Table with a very attractive female. I'm sure he wants you to come over."

Jake spotted me as I moved out of the kitchen. He motioned with his hand for me to come join them. I headed for The Table. Jake had a huge smile as he introduced me to Linda Louer. Jake stood up, reached over to my elbow, and pulled me close to Linda.

I looked at Linda.

I offered, "Hello. Very nice of you to come visit me here at Lloyd's. Where did you come from?"

"I came in yesterday from my college. I stayed with a friend on 86th and 2nd. Jake met me there."

Jake was still smiling. "She doesn't like to say Vassar. But that's where this poor girl goes."

Jake put his hand around her shoulder.

"How did you guys meet?"

I took another sip of my drink.

"I'm from Newton. I was thinking of going to Brandeis, before I decided it was too close to home. Jake was my tour guy at Brandeis. He was a sophomore at the time. He couldn't have been nicer and we've stayed in touch."

"I brought Linda here to show her what two college

boys are doing to pay the rent."

"Jake and I have noticed another Vassar girl that drops by every once in a while."

I took a swallow of the drink I had brought over to The Table. "Her name is Esther Nan Bell."

Linda smiled broadly. "I know Esther Nan very well. We went to summer camp together and ended up at the same college. Serendipity!"

I looked over at Jake. He looked puzzled and then glared at me.

"What is this? Twenty Questions??"

Jake removed his hand from around Linda's shoulder and pointed at me. "How about a little service here?"

I gazed at Linda. "What can I bring you two?"

Jake pointed at the kitchen. "We'll have three roast beefs with Russian dressing, no onions and two potato salads."

Jake smirked.

I looked at both Jake and Linda. "Why three?"

Jake spoke first, "I like the price, especially since you are not going to charge us."

Linda started to laugh. "If you must know, Mr. Busy Body, I'll bring one back to my friends. I'll explain before you ask. Why only one? My friends test everything with their dog. They watch to see how fast he gobbles the food up they put in his bowl. They actually time the dog with a stopwatch. They keep recording his times along with what they serve him."

Linda looked over at Jake who was nodding.

I thought I'd heard everything. Fred and Susan Joseph had taken home a sandwich for their dog. But at least he wasn't a taster. This made me think of Fred and Elsie's. I hadn't heard back from Fred yet. Fred was supposed to get back to me as to whether Elsie's sandwich or mine was better. Now my sandwich was going to be tested by a dog. I might as well not say another word.

I went back to the kitchen thinking I had tomorrow off. I'd go to the movies with Diane and I'd have an entire day not thinking about roast beef sandwiches.

It was getting to be closing time. I had waved goodbye to Jake and Linda as they got up to leave. Natasha came into the kitchen for her pocketbook.

I handed Natasha her purse. "See you Tuesday. Let me know what's cracking at Elaine's."

Natasha looked quite pleased. "Yeah, I'm looking forward to working there tomorrow. Try to enjoy your day off."

Natasha skipped out the door.

33

DIANE AND I GO TO THE MOVIES

I SPENT MOST of the day in my apartment reading <u>Catcher in the Rye</u>. I had read it before, but it still seemed fresh to me. I wondered if J.D. Salinger would ever visit Elaine's. I think he might have a field day with who is a phony, and who isn't. I was trying to figure out why the book was so popular. Not much happens in it. Anyway, my goal was to finish it before I'd meet Diane. I didn't. I was probably too excited. I kept getting distracted thinking about the evening.

I had picked up a *Village Voice* as I thought it might

help with my conversation with Diane. As I perused through it, I felt as if I were back at Lloyd's talking to Abbie. I had never seen anyone carry a newspaper into Lloyd's. One of the Voice's writers named Jack Newfield was describing Huntington housewives as having no thoughts or care for the world around them. The world that they didn't notice was violently exploding. What were these housewives thinking? Probably what they would be serving their husband and kids for dinner and what they would wear to the Saturday evening party. Abbie was right. Lloyd's was the same as Newfield's description of the Huntington housewives. If there was one word to describe Lloyd's, it would be apathetic. But still, I was annoyed that a supposedly "hip, liberal" columnist could generalize to such a degree about so many people that he didn't know. The phone rang.

"Hi, they rescheduled me and I'm back sooner than I thought. Watcha doing?"

Sue sounded excited.

"I'm going to a movie tonight at the Thalia theatre."

Sue laughed. "Wow! Since when do you go to movies? You've only been living on the West Side for a couple of weeks. When did you get converted? By the way, on another subject, did you pay Magda?"

"Yes, I did. Magda wouldn't let me pay for your dinner. She considered it such a treat to have someone as lovely as you visit her restaurant."

Sue sounded surprised. "That was so nice of her to

say that, but now I might be embarrassed to return. It was such an exquisite night. I'm so glad that it was just the two of us."

"You are right. It was special, as all our nights together are. By the way, do you remember Diane from the Simon and Garfunkel concert? Evidently, she is a movie aficionado. I'll be going with her to see a foreign film called *Knife in the Water*."

Sue's voice was lower. "We never needed any other entertainment but each other. That's what made us so special."

"Sue, I'm just going to a movie. I'll tell you all about it later this week."

Sue's voice was higher. "Will you tell me all about it if you sleep with her?"

I laughed. "Of course."

"I hope you enjoy the movie, Mr. West Sider."

Sue hung up her phone.

Suddenly I felt this wave of disloyalty. Sue had been my savior when I needed one the most. She cared for me in every way possible. But what was I doing wrong? I was going to a bloody movie. We weren't married. We weren't anything except the best of friends who happened to enjoy each other's bodies.

Maybe I'd learn something, just maybe. I washed up. I gargled. I knew my breath could get pretty smelly when I lounged around reading and nibbling. I even combed my hair.

I was at the foot of Diane's steps at 6:12. Two minutes later Diane came out. She was smiling.

"Good evening, Robert. Great to see you. You look ready for a walk to the Thalia. Are you looking forward to the movie?"

I touched Diane's arm. "Yuh, I am. I can't remember seeing a movie with subtitles. I hope they'll be easy to read."

Diane sighed. "This is the Thalia Theatre. This theatre wants people to return. Thalia herself is a Greek goddess. She is known for her beauty and grace. She will do everything in her power to make you feel comfortable. And believe me, she has a lot of power."

Diane grinned as she put her hand on my elbow and looked at me expectantly.

I shrugged. "It's all Greek to me."

Diane snickered. "You can do better than that."

Diane squeezed my elbow tightly. "What's up with you and Sue? Are you an 'item' as Hollywood would say?"

"If we are talking Hollywood, I'd say we are just very good friends."

I looked over at Diane as we approached Broadway. "Sue is one of the nicest, most generous persons I've ever met. I like her more than a lot."

Diane gestured at the traffic light. "Let's cross here. It sounds serious. I mean Sue and you. What are you going to do about it?"

We began to move quickly before the light changed. As we touched down on the West Side of Broadway,

I confided, "Probably nothing. There isn't anything I can do about it. I'm too poor to get involved in anything beyond a good friendship. Also, I'm too ignorant."

Diane grimaced. "I get the poor, but not the ignorant."

I emphasized my words as I slowed our pace. "I'm not sure if you are insinuating marriage. If you are, it's a huge undertaking. You really have to know what you are doing."

Diane agreed. "You aren't mistaken. So many people our age jump into marriage with their eyes wide shut. I know my boyfriend Murray wishes he had been more careful. He has alimony and nasty conversations with his ex."

Diane shook her head and continued, "Hey, look over to your left. That's Victor's. He boasts that he has the best burger in New York City. I'm not sure he's right, but it's a damn good burger. Let's pick up a few after the movie."

I sniffed the air. "Smells delicious! We'll take them up to my place. How does that sound?"

"Deeelicious!" Diane laughed. "Did your parents have a good marriage?"

"I thought we weren't going to talk Sue or Murray. Let's not talk parents either."

Suddenly, Diane broke away. She turned to look

back at me as she scampered toward 95th.

"Let's see if a Jewish Dorchester boy can catch a swift Catholic Lowell girl!"

Diane was already about to enter the theatre.

She yelled out, "I'll buy the tickets. You buy the burgers."

She was in the lobby waiting for me. "Here's your ticket. Now I have certain movie rules. Please listen carefully. First, we are here early enough to get one aisle seat, and the one beside it. Next, I don't allow any talking. That's for later. If you have to sneeze or cough, even though there will be subtitles, I'd prefer that you walk out to the lobby. Otherwise, I'm a joy to go to the movies with, except I forgot to mention, please keep your hands to yourself. That is also for later. I have to be able to totally concentrate on the movie. Remember I told you a good movie can make me very, very horny."

We took the seats Diane pointed to. I chose the aisle seat just in case I had to sneeze or cough. It could have been the subtitles that prompted her to sit so close to the screen. Previously, I had noticed that Diane fumbled for her glasses from time to time.

We sat quietly for about ninety minutes. The subtitles were surprisingly easy to read and well timed. The actors were excellent. All three of them were very believable. Most of it took place on a so-called pleasure boat. I didn't think the movie deserved the rave reviews I had read in the lobby. It looked to me like just another story about two guys who were hoping to out macho each other in front of a beautiful woman. As we left the theatre, we walked silently for at least three blocks.

Finally, Diane glanced at me. "Whaddaya think?"

I looked over at her. I thought her face would be expressing a lot of passion. It wasn't.

"I thought the acting was good. The casting was questionable. I thought the young man looked older than nineteen. The woman was delectable. But I wished she had been more outspoken earlier."

"Robert, this director is Roman Polanski. He's very young—I think in his early twenties. I'm guessing the people that matter want to encourage him. They see talent there."

As Diane spoke, she almost came to a stop. "Look to your right. That's Starks. It's a great breakfast and lunch place. The intellectuals on the West Side love it. These couples come in with their Sunday Times. Each one takes a section. Then for the next hour or so not one word is uttered, except to order their breakfast."

I looked searchingly again at Diane. "Where is the burger place? I'm getting very hungry."

"It's the very next block. I suggest we each get two. If we don't finish them, we can have them for breakfast tomorrow."

I began picking up our pace. I wanted to get the burgers and eat at least some of them as soon as possible. "Diane, I like the idea of burgers for breakfast tomorrow. Maybe even breakfast in bed?"

Diane smiled. "Let's get to your place. Let's eat the burgers and talk a bit more about the movie. Besides, tomorrow is Monday in case you haven't noticed. I get to work at about 9:00. Jake and I have bagel break at 10:30."

We arrived at Victor's and rang the bell that was on the outside counter. A man with a striped apron appeared.

"How many you want? With onion or no onion?"

Diane touched my hand. "No onions! I speak for both of us!"

The man looked out at us. "Are you sure you don't want onions? They add a lot of flavor."

I looked back at him. "Yes, we are sure we don't want any onions, but thanks for asking."

The man's face seemed to sadden. "Okay, no onions, but you don't know what you are missing. Four burgers with no onion coming right up."

He was right. The burgers came right up. He handed me four neatly wrapped burgers. I gave two to Diane.

Diane began walking back to our street. "As I told you, I've been here many times. It's strange—he never, ever mentioned onions to me. Anyway, let's get up to your place quickly. I hate cold burgers."

We climbed the four flights in record time. We

began munching. Diane took a convincing bite as she began speaking.

"Were you impressed by the director's flair for stoking up a rivalry? I mean these two guys didn't know each other and suddenly the competition between the two of them became vicious. If you want to become a true movie buff, you have to pay close attention to the directors. You have to watch carefully for their way of telling a story."

I finished my two burgers. I looked over at Diane who was just getting to her second burger.

"I'm guessing he was trying to be somewhat subtle. But putting that beautiful body in a two-piece bathing suit, what could anyone expect?"

Diane chortled. "I love how succinctly you dissected the flick. Let me check out your bed. My theory is the sooner we get to the sex the smoother our friendship will be. But before we do, you should know that I see a shrink once a week."

I tapped the bed. "Why? Why do you see a therapist?" Diane sat down at the end of the bed. "Two reasons. The first reason is I had a really terrific boyfriend. I'm sure Jake mentioned him to you. Jake and Ivan are buddies. Ivan loved me. He truly loved me. He probably still does. I dumped him for Murray who sometimes says 'I've got shit for brains.' He is not always nice to me. Not at all like Ivan was. My therapist says I have masochistic tendencies."

I squeezed Diane's leg. "Masochism? Do you need me to spank you for being so bossy at the Thalia? What's the second reason? I hope it's a better reason than that."

"The second reason is embarrassing." Diane sighed. "My therapist insists that I'm not having a real orgasm until I have a vaginal orgasm. She says mine are merely clitoral."

"Well, you can tell your therapist that I don't have either one. Perhaps, I'd better see your shrink twice a week. Anyway, let's try for a vaginal one tonight. Maybe the burgers will help."

Diane began removing her clothes. "Robert, stop looking at me as if I were the third burger. You look like you want to devour me."

Diane wasn't wrong. She did look delicious. Her fair skin was so incredible, so beautifully smooth. I pounced on the bed.

I bragged, "I'm going to kiss your gorgeous body. I'm going to kiss it on parts you forgot you had."

When we finally released our mutual embrace, I asked a little hesitantly, "It sure sounded vaginal? What do you think?"

Diane smiled. "It was very good, but not good enough for me to fire my therapist. Not yet anyway. But who knows? It could keep getting even better?"

I murmured, "I like that kind of inspirational talk."

Diane patted my naked stomach. "Are you going to tell Sue?"

"Why do you ask? I'm pretty sure she'll call and ask about the movie. I never want to hurt Sue's feelings. She is way too nice a person."

I pressed Diane's hand against my stomach.

Diane snickered. "I will definitely not tell Murray. I know he sleeps with other women. He frequently says 'No ties.' I'd better get dressed. As I explained before, I have to get up in the morning."

Diane rose and kissed me on the forehead. "That kiss was to thank you for a lovely evening and wishing you a good night's sleep."

"I almost forgot to wish you a vaginal orgasm the next time we make love."

I reached out to touch her as she began dressing.

"Thank you. It was the best!"

34

THE LAST SANDWICH

THE NEXT MORNING at about 11:00, I arrived at Lloyd's. I couldn't believe my ears. The jukebox was blaring out *Will You Still Love Me Tomorrow?* I knew that a young girl named Carole King had written it. Brilliant, I thought. It doesn't have to be exclusive for women. We guys want to know as well. I thought that Carole King was asking for a lot with the word "love." If I had the brilliance to have written it, I would have phrased it *Will You Still **Like** Me Tomorrow?*

Meg arrived early. She was smiling. She had on her brightest smile.

"Robert, hope you had a nice Sunday off. What did ya do?"

"I went to the movies with a friend."

Meg looked curious. "A guy friend? What movie?"

I smiled back at Meg. "That's two questions. Which one do you want answered first?"

I was teasing Meg. I was sure she thought I was a "swinger" after what Charlie had to say.

"I went with a girl I had met at a Simon and Garfunkel concert. We went to a movie theatre called The Thalia that specializes in foreign movies. The movie was *Knife in the Water*."

Meg seemed interested. "Was the movie any good?" I knew that Meg really didn't care about the movie.

She really wanted to know about Diane. I swung into the kitchen and Meg followed.

"Meg, I know you were here yesterday. Any more Charlie news?"

Meg's smile broadened. She knew something I didn't know.

"Yes, I'm sure you heard that Charlie and Gloria are discussing major changes. Nobody seems to know what they are. The latest news is they are returning tomorrow, not Wednesday. We had all heard Wednesday."

I shook my head as I washed my hands. "That is news. I won't even begin to ask why they changed their date. Hard people to figure."

Meg tightened her apron and laughed. "Charlie and I have been good friends for at least two years. I like him a lot, but I never try to figure him out. That's probably why we are such good friends."

I turned to check the bar. The jukebox was playing *Wings of a Dove* by Ferlin Husky. Skip and Dick were sitting on their usual bar stools. I waved at them and they both motioned me to join them. I'd try later. I fondled the now-found vodka bottle. I was very excited to show it to Charlie.

After cutting up a ton of sandwiches that I passed over to Meg, I decided to take a breather. I sidled over to Dick and Skip. Skip looked very excited.

"I'm bringing Daryl here tomorrow evening. Things are looking very promising for us."

Skip seemed to glow.

"Remember I mentioned her to you."

Dick's grin was ear to ear. He really did look like Clark Gable when he smiled like that.

"I met her. You'll like her. I know I do."

"Congrats to you both. Coming out of this crazy time with some future stability is quite an achievement."

I gave them both my highest high fives.

Dick took a sip of his beer. "We heard Charlie and Gloria are returning tomorrow. We hope you aren't concerned. We've both told Charlie how much we like you and your food."

I gave Dick a thumbs up. "I've got to get back to the kitchen before Meg gets upset."

It was another decent evening. All went smoothly.

I returned to my apartment about 11:00. As I walked in, the phone was ringing.

"Hi, it's Sue. Who else would call you at this hour? I'm stuck out here in freezing ass Chicago. How was the movie?"

I put the phone close to my ear. "I don't know how I'd rate it. I'm still thinking about it."

"Well, I thought Diane was a huge movie goer. Like she knew a lot about movies. What was her opinion?"

Sue sounded puzzled. Now I was puzzled. Diane hadn't really made clear whether she liked the movie or not. She had spoken mostly about getting familiar with directors. Besides Sue, like Meg, really didn't give a damn about the movie. She wanted more info on Diane. I was sure Sue was mostly interested to know if we had slept together. I decided to just blurt it out and get it over with. "After the movie we picked up some burgers on Broadway. We took them back to my apartment, finished them off, and had sex."

There was a long silent moment.

"I thought you would. I remember Diane as very pretty. I remember that as little as we spoke, I liked her. I wouldn't say you have my blessings, but she is a lot better than some of those girls at Lloyd's who've looked at you that special way."

I held the phone even closer. "Thank you for being you."

Sue breathed heavily into her phone. "Thank you

for being honest. But I'm still not going to move over to your roof."

I heard her familiar laughter.

"Anyway, Robert, it's late. We both better get some sleep."

***

I arrived at Lloyd's a little before noon the next day. Charlie wasn't there yet. I went directly into the kitchen and grabbed the newly found vodka bottle. I couldn't wait to show Charlie. I heard some buzzing over the jukebox that was playing *Sad Movies* (*Make Me Cry*). I looked out at the bar and both Charlie and Gloria were there. They seemed to be whispering to each other. Charlie headed to the kitchen. He seemed anxious as he acknowledged me.

I looked up at Charlie. "I've got great news. Jake and I found the bottle of vodka you left here. It was under a pile of clutter."

I proudly handed Charlie the bottle. "Here it is."

Charlie looked at it with disdain. "This isn't the same bottle. You stole the bottle I left. You replaced it with this piece of garbage. Robert, you are a dishonest person. Gloria says your salad dressings are too good not to be fattening. You were also not honest about you and Meg when you showed her your apartment. Even your brother says that you both make up stories. I want you to get out of here!"

I stared at Charlie. I tried to speak, but no words

came out.

He's not well. He's REALLY not well. Why would anyone steal a bottle of vodka and then replace it with the same one? Why? Why??

I left. I walked slowly over to Brandy's. My ears were ringing. I couldn't believe what I had just heard. I now had no job. I had no money. I had no franchise deal. I had nothing. What was I going to do?

When I arrived, Arnie and Bobby Hebb were in some kind of a huddle. They both turned to look at me.

Arnie grinned. "What brings you here so early in the day? I'd been hoping to see you. I mentioned that to Jake a week ago."

I was shaking all over. I could barely say the words.

"Charlie threw me out."

Arnie could barely contain himself. "What are you going to do?"

I had to give Arnie credit. He didn't say I told you so.

I looked back at the two of them.

"I'm not sure."

Arnie looked into the kitchen.

"I don't intend to put in a stove. It would be too cumbersome. We'll probably switch to burgers. We could just cook those up on a griddle. Would you want to call it 'Robert's Fairly Famous Burger'?"

I shuffled my feet. "I think not. I just wanted to

break the news before you heard it from someone else."

I reached out to shake their hands and say goodbye. All I could manage was a whispered, "Good luck."

I went back to my apartment. I took another shower. I felt unclean. I began searching for the business cards Sue had given me. Right at the top was Eric J. Metzger's.

I called his New Jersey number. My hands were shaking as a woman answered.

"May I speak to Mr. Metzger?"

"Whom may I say is calling?" the woman asked.
"Please tell Mr. Metzger, Robert Isenberg."

"I'll put him on," she uttered officiously.

"And just who is Robert Isenberg?" Eric seemed to be smiling into the phone.

I was unnerved, but I responded, "Do you remember a stewardess named Sue? She was one of the flight attendants on your TWA flight back to Newark. You were coming back from an appointment that you had at Sears that day. You mentioned to her that you were always looking for young men to work with. I'm one young man who would very much like to meet you."

"How is a week from Friday at about 12:00 p.m.? Let's set up a lunch date. I'll interview you while we eat. You'll see. I never like to lose even a minute. I'm going to order Provolone and Prosciutto sandwiches for both of us."

Sue had mentioned that her breasts, or should I say her beautiful little 'uppies,' weren't Kosher. I certainly liked them very much. Clearly Eric's food preferences weren't Kosher. Maybe I'll become fond of him as well?

Eric murmured, "Who could forget Sue?"

EPILOGUE

I loved these friends at the time I knew them. I had no idea who they would one day become.

- Pat Steinberger: Please see the book <u>Why Men Are Suspicious of Yoga, Some Funny & Some Not So Funny</u> Stories. You'll see why in: THE APOLOGY
Sue mentioned that she had a feeling Pat would one day apologize to me.
- Jake Katz was a wonderful friend, always present whenever someone needed a friend. Jake passed away from Alzheimer's at the Hebrew Rehab in Roslindale, Massachusetts on 9/3/2015.
- Ira Landess died on 01/02/2014 while trying bravely to save his wife and dog, both of whom had fallen through the ice and were drowning in a pond that was on their property. Ira had been a teacher in New York City. He evolved to becoming a psychotherapist. He was adored by his many

students, clients, and friends as well as his children and grandchildren.
- Fred Joseph died on 11/27/2009. He rose to become the CEO of Drexel Burnham. Fred was Mike Milken's boss. The rest of the Fred Joseph story can be found in this book's addendum. Fred never said whose sandwich was better: Elsie's or "Robert's Fairly Famous."
- Jimmy Breslin did write a book about Branch Rickey. Please find my essay profiling Branch Rickey in the book Why Men Are Suspicious of Yoga, Some Funny & Some Not So Funny Stories.
- Frank became engaged to Nina. He set up a connection between me and Esther Nan. Esther Nan and I attended their wedding. A few years later, we married. Frank became a successful banker and venture capitalist. He and Nina have a private compound where they enjoy wonderful times with children and grandchildren. There was every reason to believe that Frank would be successful in everything he did.
- Esther Nan went from Esther Nan Bell to Esther Bell Isenberg. Esther Bell Isenberg is the mother of our two daughters, Sarah and Rebeca, my business partner, and has taught yoga for more than thirty years. There is a comment in Wham Bam! about how frightening it would be to be married to a Yoga teacher. I was very wrong! Esther adores being a grandmother to Finleigh, Freya and Gloria. She has helped with many of the aspects of publishing my writings. Many references to our ongoing connections can be found throughout tales in the

book <u>Why Men Are Suspicious of Yoga, Some Funny & Some Not So Funny Stories</u>, where Esther appears as "Dana," who is similar, but as Esther prefers to think, not quite the same.
- Ronnie was the girl Peter lost to the University of Michigan. She came back and they married. They are still very beautifully together. Peter invented a product for the shoe and auto seat business. He became the CEO of a supply company that went public very successfully.
- Sue married a prominent lawyer and as far as I know has lived happily ever after. At least, I hope so.
- My sister Charlotte is featured in the book, <u>Why Men Are Suspicious of Yoga, Some Funny & Some Not So Funny Stories</u> in a tale called "Foul Weather Friends."
- My brother David had married Lorraine Gold, Diane's mentor. The story about my brother David and his marriage to Lorraine comes up in the story "Brothers" in <u>Why Men Are Suspicious of Yoga, Some Funny & Some Not So Funny Stories,</u> and Dana and I begin to say goodbye to him in "Learning How to Just Watch."
- My brother "Paul's Special Birthday" can be found in the Family Section of <u>Why Men Are Suspicious of Yoga, Some Funny & Some Not So Funny Stories.</u>
- "Robert's Fairly Famous" turned down the franchise offer. The offered deal may have developed into Arby's, now worth about eleven billion dollars. However, like most businesses, Arby's had a rocky road to get to where it is now. It's easy to second guess, but in truth, we'll never know what might have been or if the franchise offer actually came

from what became Arby's. Today Arby's is owned by a company called Inspire. Inspire bills itself as the second largest restaurant company in the USA based on sales of about twenty-five billion a year. They also own Dunkin Brand formerly known as Dunkin Donuts.
- I did take a sociology class from Ernest van den Haag. He had much to say about many things, including the attraction between Jewish men and Gentile women. He did write the book <u>The Jewish Mystique</u>.
- Elaine's was a hang-out for young writers, who in turn attracted celebrities and gawkers. It was their Algonquin. Tom Wolfe was a major player there. He wrote many best sellers. Pete Hamill escorted Jackie Kennedy frequently to Elaine's. Elaine Kaufman, the owner, chased away the notorious paparazzo, Ron Galella, as she called him a "creep" and threatened him with the lid of a garbage can.
- In a letter to Elaine, Norman Mailer swore he would never go back to Elaine's. Elaine said Mailer was boring. Woody Allen was one of her favorites. He received special treatment there. He repaid her by having the opening scene of the movie "Manhattan" take place at Elaine's.

    When someone wanted to know where the men's room was, Elaine would say, "Take a right at Michael Caine's table."
- I, myself, have gawked at various celebrities at compelling moments, such as when Jackie was crossing Fifth Avenue to a suddenly silent City. I have presented some of these events in my story

"Gawkers" as published in <u>Why Men Are Suspicious of Yoga, Some Funny & Some Not so Funny Stories.</u>
- Many years beyond the Sixties, when my daughter was attending N.Y.U., I revisited Elaine's. I shuffled over to her. I reminded her that we had met many years before. She squinted and asked, "So what have you done since?" as she leered at me.
- Frank McCourt claims to have opened the first singles bar. It was on 3rd Avenue in N.Y.C. He named it Malachy's. Frank wrote a very successful book called <u>Angela's Ashes</u>. His younger brother's name was Malachy. He was named after their dad Malachy McCourt. Malachy ran a losing campaign for governor against Elliot Spitzer.
- I just watched *Chicago Seven* with my wife Esther. We both agreed that they missed the Abbie I knew and had described to Esther. For some reason they gave Sasha Cohen a phony Boston accent. The movie did show Abbie opposing any administration that favored an unjust war.

I personally never met anyone as charismatic as Abbie Hoffman. The movie character had little charisma or none. Abbie was always an experience. When he entered a room, he lit it up. Abbie did write the book <u>Steal This Book</u> that he promised he'd write. Many potential readers took his advice and stole the book. Bookstores stopped carrying it for that reason. In November 1986, Hoffman was arrested along with fourteen others, including Amy Carter, the daughter of President Jimmy Carter. Abbie acted as his own attorney. He frequently quoted Thomas Paine, arguably the most outspoken and farsighted of the

leaders of the American Revolution. One example, "When our country is right, keep it right; but when it's wrong, right those wrongs." On April 15, 1987, the jury found Hoffman and other defendants not guilty. Abbie died alone at the age of fifty-two.
- Robert, the founder of Robert's Fairly Famous Roast Beef, after getting fired by Charlie, the manager of Lloyd's, went to work as a salesman for a boot factory. Later he and his wife Esther opened an office in Shanghai, China. There Robert designed many different types of shoes and boots. The company was called Right Stuff, Inc. using Robert's actual initials: R.S.I. The company was able to obtain six patents, not easily done with shoes and boots. Esther was the treasurer of the company and still is. She is Robert's treasure.
- Robert under the name "robear" has performed at many venues including many senior residencies. He performs many of his own essays. These pieces can be found in the book <u>Why Men Are Suspicious of Yoga, Some Funny & Some Not So Funny Stories</u>.
- Skip Kessler married Daryl. They have a son named Andrew. I'm sure they are doing quite well.
- Dick Mayer married Beverly. They have a daughter named Jessica. I hope that their lives have brought them the kind of joy they brought to others with their generous smiles and delightful ways.
- Diane Bishop interviewed Diane Keaton. She said that Diane Keaton was a delight and beautiful inside and out. Not sure if Diane was able to finally curtail her costly psychiatric visits by actually having a vaginal orgasm. I'm rooting for her. Diane Bishop

was also a delight, both inside and out.
- Brandy's Piano Bar is still at 235 East 84th Street. Fans of the place are still going through Facebook or Zoom since they cannot physically attend because of the virus. The reviews are almost all more than favorable. I heard when they were open, they were still serving burgers, but never "Fairly Famous" Burgers.
- Bobby Hebb died 8/3/2010. He was an American R & B and soul singer. He became well known for his 1966 hit titled *Sunny*.
- More about Robert's family can be found in <u>Why Men Are Suspicious of Yoga, Some Funny & Some Not So Funny Stories.</u> There is a tribute to his brother Paul on his eightieth birthday. The Car Ride depicts the effort initiated by my brother Lou's inside info, to say goodbye to Hank before he left for France in an Army Air Force B26. Enjoy breakfast on Father's Day with Robert's mother-in-law who is thriving at ninety-eight. He plans on including her in his will. Various adventures in Delray Beach, Florida are also featured. Look out for Mr. Fridge. He will be your guide.

ADDENDUM

FRED

Fred is dead! Fred owes me ten dollars. Fred and I made a bet. Whoever died first owed the other ten dollars. Fred lost!! I hope it takes a lot of time before I collect. I know Fred is waiting for me somewhere. I'm also sure he will come up with a reason why he doesn't owe me the ten dollars.

Fred and I met when we were both nine, or so he said. I didn't like Fred much back then. I thought he was a bragger and didn't think he was that good at anything.

Fred was the worst athlete of all of us. I didn't like his dog Friskie, or his squirty younger brother Stevie. I not only didn't like his mother, I feared her.

When any of us guys tried to call on Freddy to join the game, Fred's mother answered the door. Her arms were folded like an iron gate. She never asked what we wanted. She just would say, "Fred has to study. Go away!" It was difficult for Fred to improve his athletic ability, since his mother would seldom let Fred join us.

Fortunately for us, we only called on Fred when we were short a player, and that was rarely.

As we got older, now in our teens, Fred would join us on my porch. Most of us talked about the games we had played that day. When we discussed girls or women, it was with longing and despair. We talked mostly about our friends' mothers, when those friends weren't there. We were certain they were available to us. We just had to ask the right way. We also liked that their mothers had done it. Their kids were living proof.

Fred was the only one who claimed he was getting it, "regularly!!" We hated him for it. Fred also claimed that when he was eight, a twelve-year-old girl babysitter had raped him. We hated him for that too. We called him a liar. I hated him because my older sister said Fred was handsome.

Fred got a job at the local Sunoco Service Station. Fred constantly bored us with how all the girls who came into the station asked Fred out. That wasn't bad enough. We also had to hear about how strong Tim was and how large Tim's muscles were.

Tim was a black guy who had been working at the Sunoco Station for a couple of years and was showing Fred the ropes. Fred began showing us his newly found muscles. He said that in a short time he would be as strong as Tim.

Fred was still lousy at sports. In fact he was so lousy that he had to go out for track. Worse yet, it was long distance! Nobody ran long distance in those days, only guys who couldn't make any real sports teams. We associated long distance track with boredom and guys who probably liked to talk to themselves.

Fred got into Harvard. I didn't. Fred knew what he wanted to do. I didn't. Fred talked non-stop about the greatness of his new Harvard friends. We didn't know any of them, but we disliked them as much as we disliked Fred Fred and I went on a double date. My date liked Fred better than me.

Fred was discharged from the Navy, where he had served as an officer on a battleship. I was doing my worst at trying to stay awake during medic training at Fort Sam in San Antonio, Texas.

Somehow, someway, we both ended up in NYC. Fred was in Brooklyn. I was in Manhattan. Fred was married. I wasn't. I was floundering in and out of relationships. Sometimes I did the dumping. Sometimes I was dumped. Fred was delighted that I was single and going out with a lot of women. Most of them were very pretty which enhanced Fred's delight. He loved to ask each of them what such a beautiful girl was doing with me. He thought that was very funny. I didn't.

Fred had also instructed his wife to make sure that when they went out with another couple that the woman would be pretty. He told me that everybody talks about the same things so that at least, if the woman sitting across from him were pretty, the evening wouldn't drag.

Fred was working for E.F. Hutton as an investment banker. He was working for John Shad who would one day be the head of the S.E.C. Fred idolized Shad. All I heard was Shad this and Shad that. Fred had a way of making you feel that whoever he was speaking about was far better than you. This always brought back my old nasty feelings about Fred.

Fred's wife Sue was madly in love with Fred, ridiculously proud of him. She would even make the fatal error of coming to Fred's side when I attacked him. I had carefully instructed any woman that I brought to Fred and Sue's house that any defense of me would be a sign of weakness on my part.

I actually saw her shine Fred's shoes one morning, after I stayed over. We all had too much to drink the night before. This was after Sue had given birth to two girls. Fred had wanted boys. He wanted another chance to relive those childhood years that he felt his mother had cheated him out of. Fred wanted to play ball with his son. Fred wanted to hunt with his son. He wanted to teach him all the things he had learned about hunting and fishing. Most of all, when his son's friends came to call, he wanted his son to run out to play.

Things were changing for me. I was involved in an up and down relationship with a woman named Dana. Most of the downs were her parents. They had interfered with most of her previous relationships. The reason usually had been religion. In my case it was personal. It seemed unlikely to me that Dana and I would get much further than having some wonderful times together that would always be blemished by her incurable need to please her parents.

Dana and I were dining at our favorite restaurant, her apartment in Jamaica Plain. Dana looked up at me and asked if I was ever going to ask her to marry me.

I said, "Yes, I'm asking you to marry me."

Dana paused. "I don't know."

"WHAT!!" I screamed.

Dana said, "It's not going to be easy to tell my parents."

"Never mind your parents, I'm going to have to tell Fred," I said.

At the time, I was making a joke.

Dana and I were making wedding plans. Fred was constantly asking me why I was giving up the splendid life of a NYC bachelor. Fred often repeated his backhanded compliment. "I don't know how somebody like you could come up with so many good-looking women."

I generally responded with, "Easy."

I decided it was time for Fred and Sue to meet Dana. We had barely gone through the introductions, when Sue smiled at Dana and then at me and said, "Her parents are right. She is way too good for you." Fred was nodding in agreement.

Dana and I rented an incredible apartment on East. 54th. Life was good for us except Robert Kennedy was shot in Los Angeles while I was painting the apartment in NYC. Soon after, Richard Nixon was elected President, but aside from politics and assassinations, we were having a love affair with the city. This affair included all the ups and downs that come with most affairs.

I decided to quit the job I had been at for almost five years. The same week Fred decided to leave E.F. Hutton and go to work for Shearson, another investment banking firm. I had agreed to go to work for a company based in New Hampshire. I was somewhat depressed and very concerned about taking on a new job. Fred was somewhat anxious as well. Fred decided to rent a sixty-five-foot sail boat and he decided that Dana and I would serve as his crew. None of us had sailed before.

None of us knew anything about manning even a small sailboat, never mind this behemoth. Fred advised us that he had purchased a pamphlet called "How to Keep A Sail Boat Afloat." Besides Fred pointed out, we could stop worrying about our new jobs. Now we should be worrying, if we would come back alive.

Dana and I decided it was time to return to the Boston area. We had a six-month-old baby named Sarah. We were absolutely sure she had been conceived on the sixty-five-foot sailboat. We also had a white West Highland Terrier named Honky. Our apartment was too small and the city was too big. It was time to leave.

We cautiously looked for the right town and house to move to. We found Newburyport, or as one veteran Newburyporter told us years later, Newburyport found us. He claimed none of us came there. He said that we were all sent.

We purchased a house that had been built in the 1600s. This house had everything—everything wrong. However, it was not without its charms.

It had original beams in many of the rooms. Many of the rooms had the original wide floorboards described as King George boards. There were six fireplaces.

One gigantic fireplace was at least five feet tall. We redid the kitchen. We decided on a butcher block for all of our counters. The counters looked great and, of course, I mentioned this to Fred. This may have prompted Fred to visit us almost immediately. As soon as Fred and Sue entered the kitchen, Fred told Sue to take out her measuring tape and measure our butcher block. Fred wanted to make sure that he had more butcher block in their kitchen than we had.

Fred worried a lot about his Jewishness. He described his mother as the typical overbearing Jewish mother. Sue's mother was Jewish, her father was Catholic. Sue had been brought up Catholic. Sue's dad did not like Jews much.

Fred's mother hated Sue. Sue hated Fred's mother. Fred was quite anxious to keep me abreast of both his business accomplishments and his private life. Fred had taken to sending us photos of his various doings. There was one of Fred on his new chopper.

There was another with Fred in a tree holding a bow and arrow. He was waiting for a deer to stroll by. He claimed that using a bow and arrow, rather than a rifle, was a fairer game. Sue could be seen in the photo sitting under the tree. Sue's job was to help spot any deer Fred didn't see. We especially loved the one with Fred on his huge tractor getting ready to work his three-hundred acre farm. There would usually be a caption under all the photos that said, "This is not the way most Jewish guys relax."

Although we had moved to Boston, I still had a lot

of customers in New York City. I traveled to New York every other week and most often met Fred for dinner. After dinner and a lot of "What do you want to do??" quite often we ended up on 42nd in time to catch a pornographic film. We were watching a western porno, when Fred grabbed my arm and said the hero is Jewish.

I said, "How do you know?"

He said, "I can tell by the way he makes love."

I didn't bother pursuing his theory. Maybe he was right, and I should have paid better attention.

After dining one evening, Fred told me he had bought tickets to a live porno show for us. Neither of us had ever been to one of these before. We went. It was an interesting experience. There was quite a bit of flagellation. There was also quite a bit of dialogue. The players felt responsible to keep us informed of not only what they were doing, but what other porno theatres were doing. The Headmaster, as he referred to himself, explained to the audience that there was another live show a few blocks away. He described their theatre as being crude. He said, "Those are the kind of people that give flagellation a bad name."

Fred called the next day to say he was working with two big-name companies putting together a huge deal, but all he could think about was making plans to go to the place that was giving flagellation a bad name. We could not stop laughing.

Fred had begun to call me on a regular basis. A shoe company had come to his investment banking company and had requested startup capital. Fred wanted as much information as I could give him regarding the main man. As it happened, I knew quite a bit about him. I had been very friendly with his brother Leo. Leo had often spoken about his brother Joe and how much he admired him. I had very high regard for Leo. I trusted his insights and his opinions. Leo frequently said that Joe was the most talented and creative person he knew. I passed this information on to Fred.

Fred's company Shearson did the deal. Joe made millions. Leo made millions. Joe's company made millions. Fred and Shearson made millions. I didn't make a nickel.

Many years later I ran into Joe in an Italian Trattoria outside of Florence, Italy. I walked over to the bar and introduced myself to Joe Famolare.

I said, "I was the guy who recommended you to E.F. Hutton to help you get the start-up money."

Joe snickered. "It wasn't Hutton," he said. "It was Shearson."

I had forgotten that Fred had left E.F. Hutton, when he did the deal with Joe. I was wrong and embarrassed.

Fred left Shearson and joined Drexel Burnham as

their C.E.O. Drexel was a young investment banking company that specialized in junk bonds. Fred's first major move was to hire a highly touted junk bond specialist named Michael Milken: Fred's newest hero.

Dana and our kids loved to visit Fred and Sue's farm. It was over three-hundred acres. It was stocked with real animals. Vegetables and fruit were growing everywhere. In fact, it was a serious farm that Fred and Sue worked together. Fred would be on his tractor turning the soil. All the kids and Dana would be picking blueberries for Sue's amazing farm-made blueberry pie which we would have for dessert.

Fred loved to walk with me after dinner. He loved to tell me how much fun he was having at work. He especially loved to go on about Mike Milken. According to Fred, Milken was the most brilliant person he had ever met. According to Fred, there was nobody else in the world that could compare to Mike Milken.

"All Mike wants to do is become the richest man in the universe," Fred said.

"How rich is he now?" I asked.

"About five hundred million. He doesn't sleep. He works all night. He is working now, even though it's Sunday. I'm sure he's plotting a strategy, that he will unfold on me when I get to the shop on Monday."

This was a new world for Fred. This was the true

high life. This was a world even Fred could not have dreamt about, even in his wildest dreams. There were parties. The parties were lavish. There were celebrities seeking information. There were Wall Streeters seeking celebrities. There were lots of pretty girls. Nobody ever, ever brought their wives.

Fred fell in love. Her name was Linn. Fred wanted me to meet Linn. Her home was in the Boston area, which meant that Fred would be travelling to Boston regularly. He often called me and invited me to join them. It was always at one of the fanciest hotels in Boston. The food was invariably great as were the conversations. Fred wanted to share his world with both Linn and me.

It was exciting to hear the stories about Ted Turner. Fred described almost verbatim how Ted Turner had roasted him on Fred's fiftieth birthday.

"Ted Turner?" I said. "He doesn't know shit about you! He doesn't know that of all of us kids growing up, you were the biggest asshole. He doesn't know that you wouldn't be here posing as a big shot investment banker, if it weren't for the weekly poker games at my house. That's where you learned to cheat! You finally figured out that everybody was cheating. That's what prepared you for Wall Street, not Harvard. Turner may have roasted you! I would have fried your ass like fried chicken."

I had to admit it was exciting to hear what Fred had said to Carl Icahn. Better yet, to hear Fred tell us that he told Donald Trump that he didn't feel comfortable doing business with him. He told us who the bad boys were and who wore the white hats. At least, according to Fred.

I told Linn, "Fred wasn't smart enough to be a real bad guy. He was just a sort of a bad guy."

Drexel quickly became the most talked about company of the era. This was true on Wall Street and on Main Street. These C.E.O.s were making headlines. Fred was on the cover of quite a few weekly magazines. Drexel was growing a reputation for being very aggressive and extremely successful. Perhaps too aggressive, and way too successful.

This information did not elude the S.E.C. or the Feds. The Fed's word for aggressive was arrogant and their objective was to bring Drexel down.

Fred's oldest daughter was getting married. Her wedding took place at the farm. It was a beautiful day.

It was a beautiful setting. The guests not only looked rich, they were rich and a lot of them famous. Fred's mom and dad were there. His mom remembered me and came over to speak to me. She inquired about my dad ,who had since died, and after a few more questions, she looked around at the magnificence and said, "I did this! I did all of this."

Michael Milken went to jail kicking and screaming that it was all Fred's fault. He wrote a book calling Fred the worst liar in the country. He called Fred a gangster and said he was a member of a vicious gang growing up. The gang Milken was referring to was our club called the Vikings. Our most vicious acts were playing pinball, reading porno books in the soda fountain store behind the owner's back, and talking about the local females. We also tended to double dribble, when we played basketball. Double dribbling is considered a very serious offense in pro-basketball. Oh yeah, and there was that stuff about everybody cheating at poker.

Fred was also being tried. Tried in court and pursued by the FBI. Susie said when the family was out, the FBI was cutting down tree branches, so that they would get better tapping reception. Fred called me after his first day in court to tell me that his judge was beautiful. He said that I should definitely come to his trial and check out the judge.

"You've always needed to be judged," I said. "I don't. Besides I saw her picture somewhere recently and she's not that hot. Since you turned fifty your taste has gone south!"

During the trial, while at recess, the court journalist came over to Fred and introduced herself to him. Fred called the following week to brag, that he now had a mistress named Melanie, who he put up in a fashionable apartment near his Manhattan office. He said that she was wicked smart and best of all not like his wife Sue, or his girlfriend Linn. Melanie asked no questions.

Linn was growing tired of having only part of Fred. She wanted Fred to divorce Sue and marry her. Fred told me he was considering doing this.

"Fred," I said, "just give me two weeks' notice. I don't want to be in the country when you tell Sue. I don't want to get hit by the shrapnel when Sue's bomb goes off."

I met Fred for dinner. I was hoping I could talk him out of leaving Sue. I understood that it wasn't easy for him to be with Sue. It hadn't been for a while. Sue had grown bitter. She didn't like the world that Fred had adopted. She didn't like Fred's business. Sue had taken on her dad's anti-semitism.

She was constantly pointing out the Jewish names, who were getting caught in one white collar crime or another. I could understand Fred wanting a younger, prettier woman, but Sue had done so much. Five kids, all raised successfully, mostly by Sue. Sue's supreme love and total loyalty to Fred had to count. Fred heard me, but he said, "I'm far richer than you, I'm much smarter than you, I'm way handsomer than you, but you have Dana and I don't." Was it possible that so much of this was about Dana, including Linn?

"My G-D," I said, "you really are a sick, crazy competitive bastard. I thought we were just having fun. I guess that's why I have Dana and you don't. Besides, neither one of us has any butcher block anymore. Get over it. We left the butcher block in Newburyport that you had Sue measure a long time ago. Nor do I really have Dana. I'm married to her."

Fred was trying to start a new investment banking company. I had begun to perform my stories at many different venues. One of these venues was the Hebrew Rehab in Roslindale, Mass. I had mentioned to Fred that I was performing at various nursing homes. I asked him if he knew Sheldon Adelson, originally from Dorchester. Sheldon had become one of the richest men in the world as owner of the Sands Company and the Venetian Hotel chain. I told Fred that Sheldon had contributed over eighteen million to the Hebrew Rehab. "Hebrew Rehab," Fred said. "That's where my mother is. I'd really appreciate if you would say hello to her. Maybe I'll send Sheldon a thank you note for helping take care of my mother. I didn't think anyone could do that. That is, take care of my mother."

On our next visit to the rehab I found Fred's mother. She didn't know me.
I said, "Fred and I were and still are friends."
"Fred?" she said. "He is my oldest. Fred is seventy-

five."

At the time Fred was sixty-three. I called Fred the next day and blasted him out for lying to me about his age, the day we first met. I was nine and he had said he was nine as well. I said, "No wonder you did so well in school. You were twelve years older than the rest of us."

Fred was a busy boy. He was contemplating how and where to tell Sue that he wanted a divorce. How close to the door should he stand, without causing too much suspicion? At the same time, he was battling the attorney general's office, maintaining his innocence, and validating his stupidity. His defense was based on his not knowing what Milken and his subordinates were doing behind his back. This seemed to qualify for gross stupidity. At the same time, he was still seeing his girlfriend and his mistress. Fred never said goodbye on the phone any longer; he would sign off by saying to me: "Stay out of trouble!"

Finally, Fred called and said he would tell Sue at the farm.

I said, "You had better wear the helmet from your motorcycle days and maybe a bulletproof vest if Sue finds your bow and arrows."

I thanked him for letting me know and said that even though I had just returned from China, I would leave for China tomorrow.

Fred did tell Sue he was leaving her. Sue did not

take it well. I actually didn't leave for China, but stayed home in Lexington. Fred delivered his message to Sue in their New Jersey home. Although it is about two hundred and thirty miles from our home to theirs, I was sure I could hear Sue's cries. I felt horrible for Sue and their five kids. Why couldn't Fred maintain the status quo? I thought he had everything he ever wanted . . . enough sex between the three women that should have satisfied even Fred.

Fred married Linn and shortly thereafter he was diagnosed with multiple myeloma. Fred, being Fred, learned as much as any doctor knew about the disease. Because Fred had a lot of money, he went to any and every hospital or clinic for hope. The generous doctors graciously gave Fred two years. Fred got over five. The week before he died, Dana and I joined Fred and Linn for dinner at Bertucci's in Andover, Mass.

Too soon after, Fred called me from the Dana Farber to inform me that he had relapsed and that it was my fault.

"Why? You can't blame me just because you have a namby pamby body, inside and out."

"I am blaming you. I'm blaming you for everything that went wrong. I just watched one of your DVDs and all I could think of is that Linn says you are handsome. I'm glad that I'm feeling well enough to tell you that I don't agree with Linn. I know handsome when I see it.

I'm handsome and you're not!!"

Fred died that day. There were two funerals, one in New Jersey and one in Andover. Linn invited Dana and me to the funeral in Andover. I called Linn to tell her that I would always be there for her.

Linn did not return my call. Nor did Fred.

Fred Joseph died November 27, 2009.

Made in the USA
Monee, IL
30 April 2021